MENSA®

MIGHTY MINDBUSTERS for KIDS

THIS IS A CARLTON BOOK

This edition published 2003

Text and puzzle content copyright © British Mensa Limited 1994, 2003
Design and artwork copyright © Carlton Books Limited 1994, 2003

A CIP catalogue for this book is available from the British Library

ISBN 1 84222 897 8
UPC 8 02880 00029 9

Printed and bound in Great Britain

MENSA

MIGHTY MINDBUSTERS for KIDS

Give your brain a workout with over 400 tricky word and number puzzles!

Robert Allen, Harold Gale & Carolyn Skitt

CARLTON
BOOKS

★ CONTENTS ★

★ INTRODUCTION ★

Here you'll find over 400 tricky word and number puzzles to give your brain a workout. They range in difficulty from the very easy (Thumb Suckers) to the difficult (Aaaargh!). But don't worry, you won't need to be a genius to solve them, all you need is a bit of logic, a little luck and great stamina. Just keep going, and you'll crack even the toughest puzzle. All these problems have been set by Mensa's team of puzzle writers, whose books have sold hundreds of thousands of copies throughout the world.

If you like puzzles, you'll like Mensa, a society that exists entirely for those who enjoy using their brains. Mensa members have one common trait: they all have an IQ in the top 2% of the nation. In the USA over 50,000 members have found out how bright they are. This leaves room for many thousands of new members. Could you make the grade?

If you enjoy mental exercise, you'll find lots of good 'workout programs' in our national monthly magazine, and you can voice your opinions in one of the many Mensa newsletters. If you want to make new friends, there are local meetings, parties and get-togethers. You can participate in lectures and debates, and attend regional meetings. There's something happening on the Mensa calendar almost daily. And Mensa is an international organisation with 100,000 members throughout the world, so there is no shortage of interesting new people to meet.

Mensa also has Special Interest Groups (SIGs) that cater for just about any interest. So whether yours is as common as crosswords or as esoteric as Egyptology, there's a SIG for it somewhere.

R. P. Allen

Robert Allen
Editorial Director
British Mensa

Here are some useful addresses:

American Mensa	Australian Mensa	Mensa International
1229 Corporate Drive	PO Box 213	15 The Ivories
West Arlington	Toorak	6-8 Northampton Street
TX 76006-6103	VIC 3142	London N1 2NY
USA	Australia	England

★ INTRODUCTION TO ★ NUMBER PUZZLES

We welcome you to the world of numbers. This part of the book has been specially written for you by Caroline Skitt and myself. The puzzles are divided into six different levels of difficulty, starting from Level A which is quite easy, to Level F which is mind-numbing!

In this section you will meet dinosaurs, zap spaceships and count coins from the distant planet of Venox. In fact, you'll have all sorts of weird and wonderful adventures. There are unusual boxes to be made, animals to trace through and flags with a difference. These puzzles, along with many, many others, will give you hours of pleasure – and that's not all. The more you use your brain the sharper it will become and so, having wandered through the easier sections, you will come up against the more difficult sections.

But how difficult are they? You will probably find them a lot easier after doing the earlier sections than they look at first sight, because you will already have had the practice. And think how pleased you'll be when you can solve puzzles that you thought were impossible.

If you would like to join Mensa, see the details on page 7.

Harold Gale
Former Executive Director of British Mensa

EASY DOES IT

★ LEVEL A ★

PUZZLE 1

Using the numbers shown how many different ways are there to add three numbers together to make a total of 8? A number can be used more than once, but a group cannot be repeated in a different order?

ANSWER NO.37

PUZZLE 2

Move up or across from the bottom left-hand 1 to the top right-hand 1. Collect nine numbers and add them together. What is the highest you can score?

ANSWER NO.169

PUZZLE 3

Join together the dots using odd numbers only.
Start at the lowest and discover the object. What is it?

A

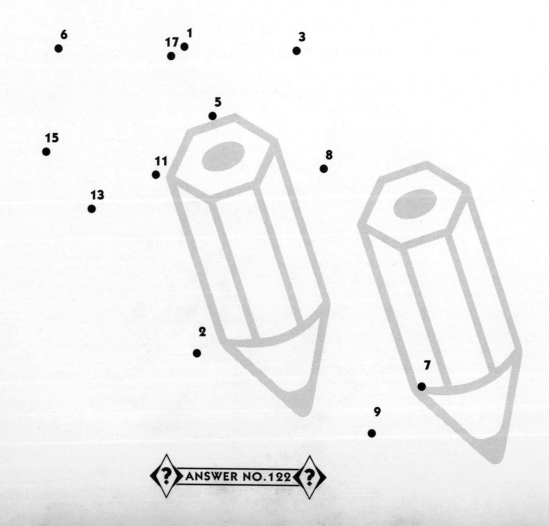

6

17 1

3

5

15

11

8

13

2

7

9

ANSWER NO.122

10

PUZZLE 4

Place in the middle box a number larger than 1.
If the number is the correct one, all the other numbers can be divided
by it without leaving any remainder. What is the number?

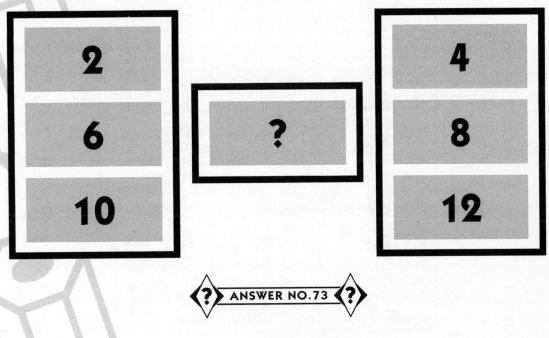

? ANSWER NO.73 ?

PUZZLE 5

Each sector of the circle follows a pattern.
What number should replace the question mark?

? ANSWER NO.145 ?

PUZZLE 6

Here is an unusual safe. Each of the buttons must be pressed only once in the correct order to open it. The last button is marked F. The number of moves and the direction is marked on each button. Thus 1U would mean one move up, whilst 1L would mean one move to the left. Which button is the first you must press? Here's a clue: it can be found on the top row.

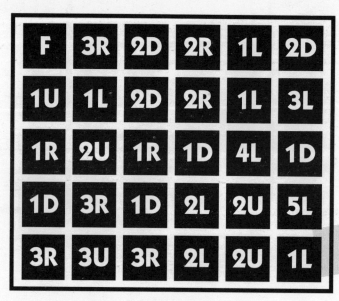

ANSWER NO.26

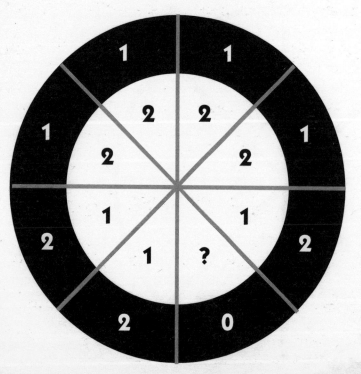

PUZZLE 7

Each slice of this cake adds up to the same number. What number should replace the question mark?

ANSWER NO.13

PUZZLE 8

Copy out these shapes carefully and rearrange them to form a number. What is it?

? ANSWER NO.196 ?

PUZZLE 9

If you look carefully you should see why the numbers are written as they are.
What number should replace the question mark?

? ANSWER NO.14 ?

PUZZLE 10

Look at the pattern of numbers in the diagram.
What number should replace the question mark?

◆? ANSWER NO.157 ?◆

PUZZLE 11

Move from the bottom left-hand 3 to the top right-hand 3 adding together
all five numbers. Each black circle is worth 1 and this should be added to your
total each time you meet one. What is the highest total you can find?

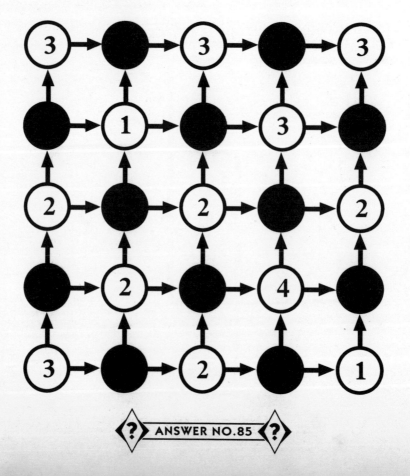

◆? ANSWER NO.85 ?◆

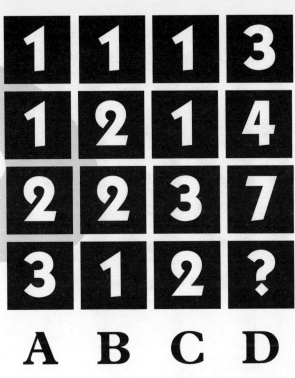

PUZZLE 12

The numbers in column D are linked in some way to those in A, B and C. What number should replace the question mark?

ANSWER NO.133

PUZZLE 13

Start at the A and move to B passing through various parts of the rhinoceros. There is a number in each part and these must be added together. What is the lowest number you can total?

ANSWER NO.62

PUZZLE 14

Each symbol is worth a number. The total of the symbols can be found alongside each row. What number should replace the question mark?

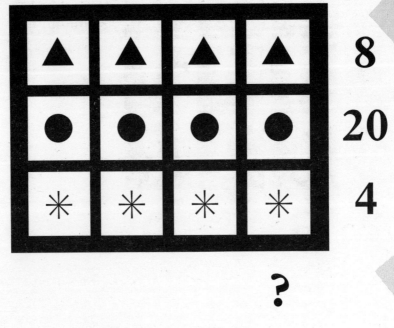

?

ANSWER NO.181

PUZZLE 15

On the planet Venox the coins used are 1V, 2V, 5V, 10V, 20V and 50V.
A Venoxian has 85V in his squiggly bank.
He has the same number of three kinds of coin.
How many of each are there and what are they?

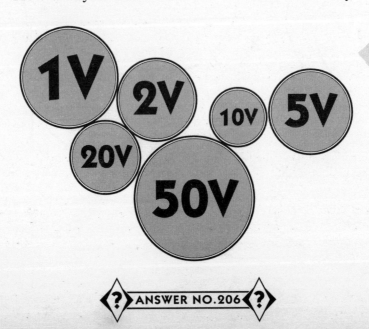

ANSWER NO.206

PUZZLE 16

What is the lowest number of lines needed to divide the camel so that you can find the numbers 1, 2 and 3 in each selection?

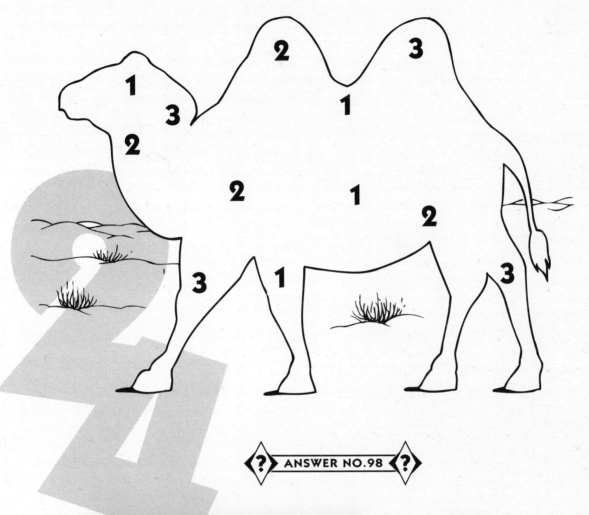

ANSWER NO.98

PUZZLE 17

1	2	3	4	5
4	5	1	2	3
2				1
		?		

Fill up this square with the numbers 1 to 5 so that no row, column or diagonal line of five squares uses the same number more than once. What number should replace the question mark?

ANSWER NO.217

17

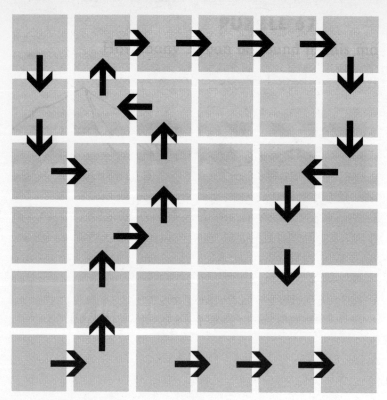

PUZZLE 18

Follow the arrows and find the longest possible route. How many boxes have been entered?

ANSWER NO.109

PUZZLE 19

The symbol on the flag will give a number. What is it?

ANSWER NO.146

A

PUZZLE 20

Start at the middle 3 and move from circle to touching circle.
Collect three numbers and add them to the 3.
How many different routes are there to make a total of 8?

ANSWER NO.25

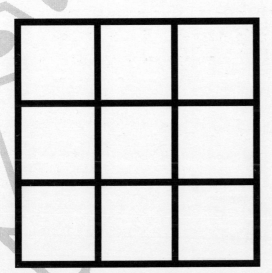

PUZZLE 21

How many squares
of any size can
you find in
this diagram?

ANSWER NO.1

The first set of scales balance.
How many A's will make the second set balance?

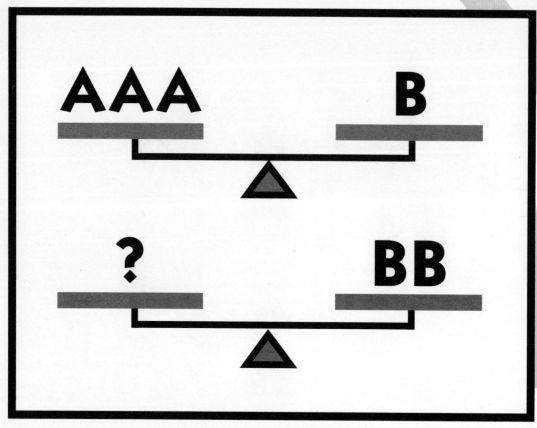

ANSWER NO.121

PUZZLE 23

Divide up the box
using four lines so that each
shape adds up to the same.
How is this done?

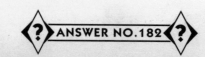

ANSWER NO.182

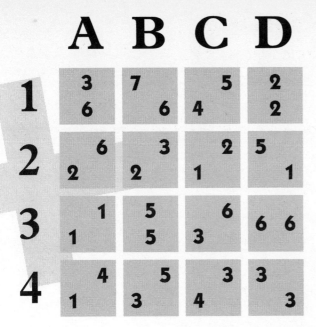

A B C D

	A	B	C	D
1	3 6	7 6	5 4	2 2
2	6 2	3 2	2 1	5 1
3	1 1	5 5	6 3	6 6
4	4 1	5 3	3 4	3 3

PUZZLE 24

Which squares contain the same numbers?

ANSWER NO.134

PUZZLE 25

Turn the number shown on the calculator into 32 by pressing two buttons only. What are they?

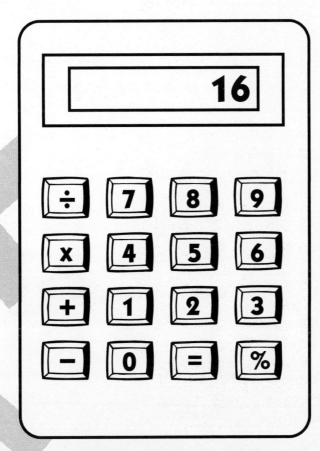

ANSWER NO.86

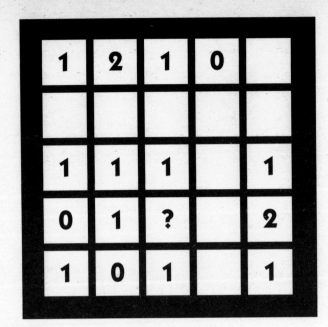

PUZZLE 26

Fill in the empty boxes so that every line adds up to 5, including the lines that go from corner to corner. What number should replace the question mark?

ANSWER NO.61

EASY DOES IT

PUZZLE 27

Copy out these shapes carefully and rearrange them to form a number. What is it?

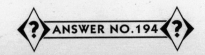
ANSWER NO.194

PUZZLE 28

Which number should be placed in the triangle to continue the series?

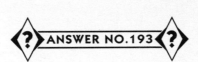
ANSWER NO.38

PUZZLE 29

Here is a series of numbers.
Which number should replace the question mark?

ANSWER NO.193

PUZZLE 30

Replace each question mark with either plus, minus, multiply or divide.
Each sign can be used more than once. When the correct ones have been used
the sum will be completed. What are the signs?

ANSWER NO.97

PUZZLE 31

Which of these pictures is not of the same box?

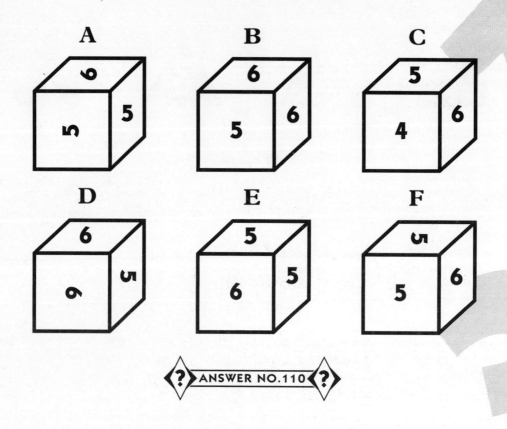

A   B   C

D   E   F

ANSWER NO.110

PUZZLE 32

How many 3's can be found in this Pterodactyl?

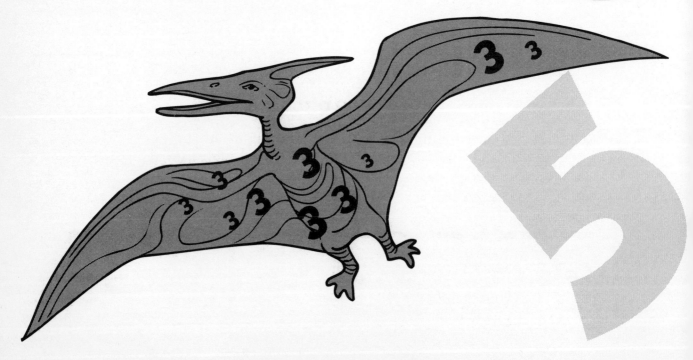

ANSWER NO.158

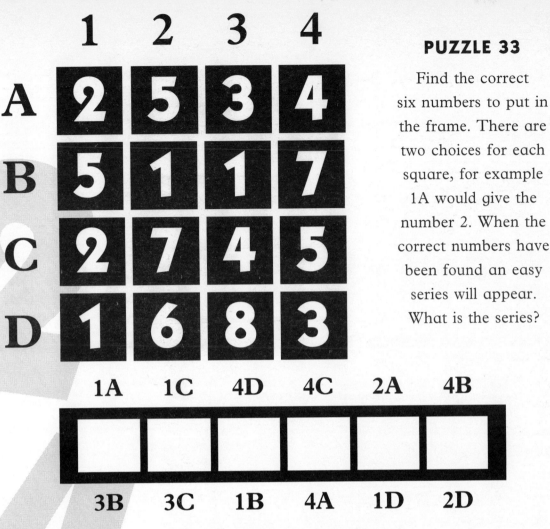

	1	2	3	4
A	2	5	3	4
B	5	1	1	7
C	2	7	4	5
D	1	6	8	3

PUZZLE 33

Find the correct six numbers to put in the frame. There are two choices for each square, for example 1A would give the number 2. When the correct numbers have been found an easy series will appear. What is the series?

1A	1C	4D	4C	2A	4B
3B	3C	1B	4A	1D	2D

ANSWER NO.205

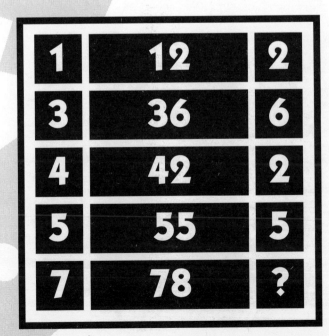

1	12	2
3	36	6
4	42	2
5	55	5
7	78	?

PUZZLE 34

The numbers in the middle section have some connection with those down the sides. Find out what it is and tell us what should replace the question mark?

ANSWER NO.2

LEVEL A

25

GETTING HARDER

★ LEVEL B ★

PUZZLE 35

The numbers in the middle section have some connection with those down the sides.
Find out what it is and tell us what should replace the question mark?

3	23	2
1	61	6
7	47	4
5	35	3
9	?	1

ANSWER NO.4

PUZZLE 36

Which number should be placed in the triangle to continue the series?

12 ? 6 3

ANSWER NO.40

PUZZLE 37

Zap the spaceship by making its number a round one. Take off either 11, 13, 19, 21 or 25 to do this. Which number ought you to use?

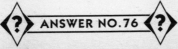

ANSWER NO.76

PUZZLE 38

Move up or across from the bottom left-hand 2 to the top right-hand 1.
Collect nine numbers and add them together. What is the highest you can score?

<ANSWER NO.171>

PUZZLE 39

Start at any corner and follow the lines. Add up the first four numbers you meet
and then add on the corner number. What is the lowest you can score?

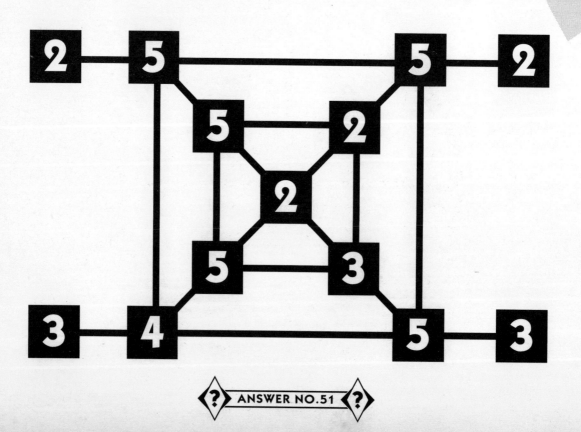

<ANSWER NO.51>

28

PUZZLE 40

Place in the middle box a number larger than 1.
If the number is the correct one, all the other numbers can be divided
by it without leaving any remainder. What is the number?

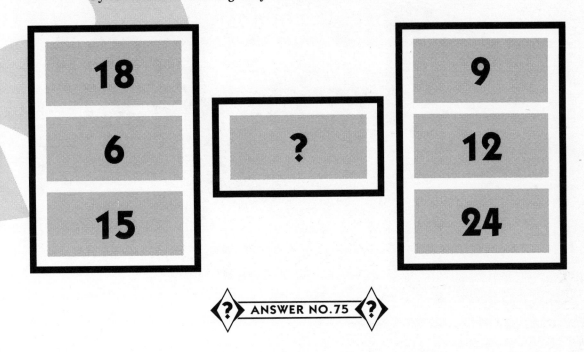

ANSWER NO.75

PUZZLE 41

Each sector of the circle follows a pattern.
What number should replace the question mark?

ANSWER NO.147

PUZZLE 42

Copy the cake slices out carefully and rearrange them to find the birthday.
How old was the birthday boy?

◇? ANSWER NO.172 ?◇

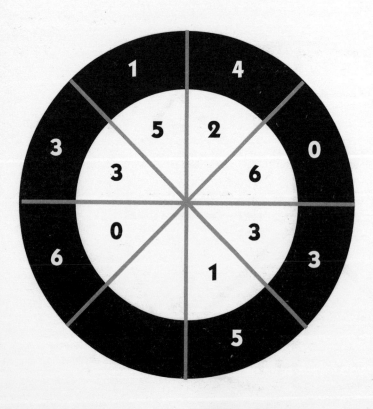

PUZZLE 43

Each slice of this cake adds
up to the same number.
All the numbers going
round the cake total 24.
Which two numbers should
appear on the blank slice?

◇? ANSWER NO.15 ?◇

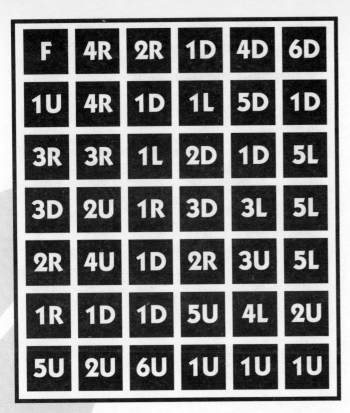

F	4R	2R	1D	4D	6D
1U	4R	1D	1L	5D	1D
3R	3R	1L	2D	1D	5L
3D	2U	1R	3D	3L	5L
2R	4U	1D	2R	3U	5L
1R	1D	1D	5U	4L	2U
5U	2U	6U	1U	1U	1U

PUZZLE 44

Here is an unusual safe. Each of the buttons must be pressed only once in the correct order to open it. The last button is marked F. The number of moves and the direction is marked on each button. Thus 1U would mean one move up, whilst 1L would mean one move to the left. Which button is the first you must press? Here's a clue: it can be found on the middle row.

ANSWER NO.28

PUZZLE 45

If you look carefully you should see why the numbers are written as they are. What number should replace the question mark?

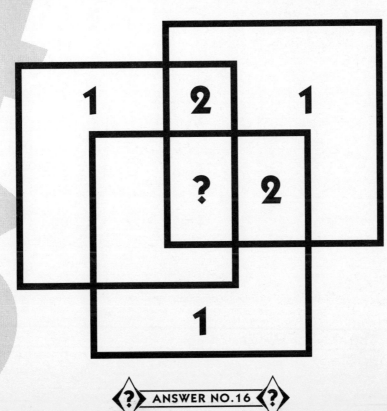

ANSWER NO.16

31

PUZZLE 46

Look at the pattern of numbers in the diagram.
What number should replace the question mark?

<?> ANSWER NO.159 <?>

PUZZLE 47

Start at the A and move to B passing through the various parts of the cat.
There is a number in each part and these must be added together.
What is the lowest number you can total?

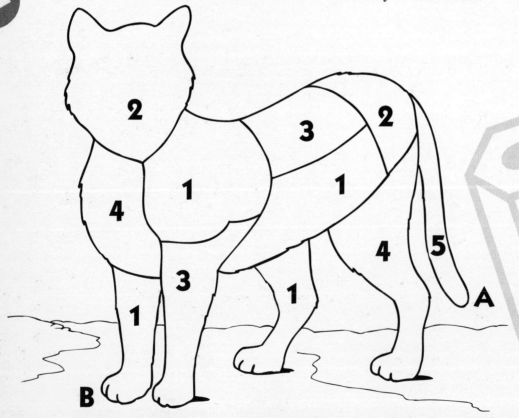

<?> ANSWER NO.64 <?>

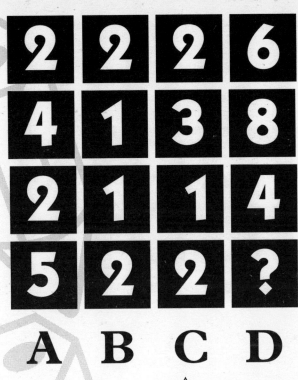

PUZZLE 48

The numbers in column D are linked in some way to those in A, B and C. What number should replace the question mark?

? ANSWER NO.135 ?

PUZZLE 49

Move from the bottom left-hand 5 to the top right-hand 2 adding together all five numbers. Each black circle is worth 2 and this should be added to your total each time you meet one. What is the highest total you can find?

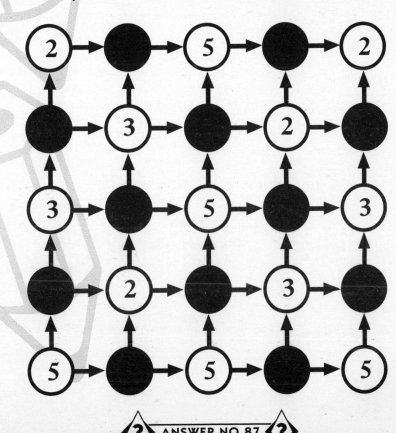

? ANSWER NO.87 ?

LEVEL B

33

PUZZLE 50

Each symbol is worth a number.
The total of the symbols can be found alongside each row and column.
What number should replace the question mark?

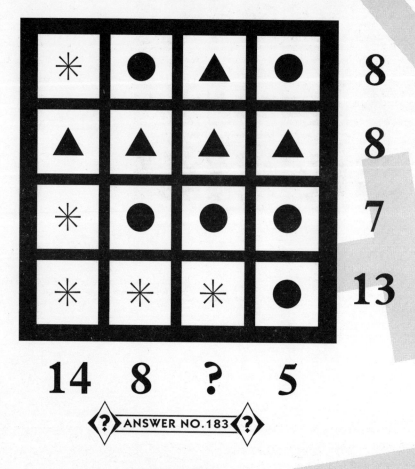

ANSWER NO.183

PUZZLE 51

On the planet Venox the coins used are 1V, 2V, 5V, 10V, 20V and 50V.
A Venoxian has 374V in his squiggly bank. He has the same number of three kinds of coin.
How many of each are there and what are they?

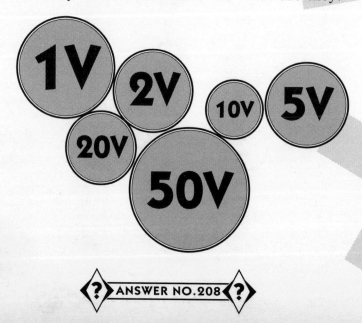

ANSWER NO.208

PUZZLE 52

What is the lowest number of lines needed to divide the elephant so that you can find the numbers 1, 2, 3 and 4 in each section?

ANSWER NO.100

PUZZLE 53

Here is a series of numbers. Which number should replace the question mark?

| 4 | 8 | 12 | 16 | 20 | 24 | ? |

ANSWER NO.195

PUZZLE 54

Replace each question mark with either plus, minus, multiply or divide. Each sign can be used more than once. When the correct ones have been used the sum will be completed. What are the signs?

| 2 | ? | 3 | ? | 1 | = | 4 |

ANSWER NO.99

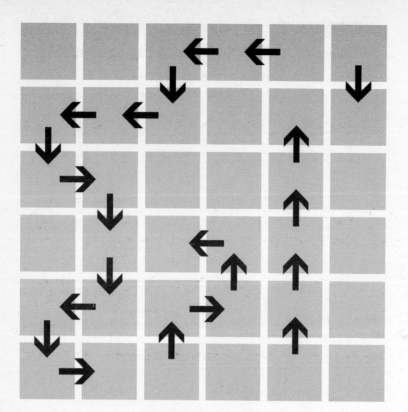

PUZZLE 55

Follow the arrows and find the longest possible route. How many boxes have been entered?

ANSWER NO.111

PUZZLE 56

The symbol on the flag will give a number. What is it?

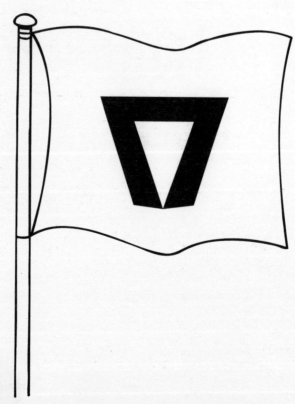

ANSWER NO.148

GETTING HARDER

B

PUZZLE 57

Start at the middle 1 and move from circle to touching circle.
Collect three numbers and add them to the 1.
How many different routes are there to make a total of 10?

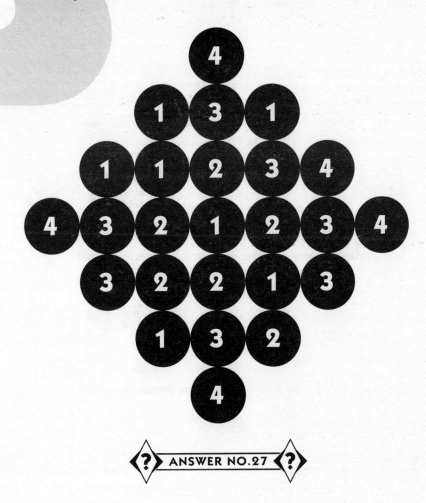

? ANSWER NO.27 ?

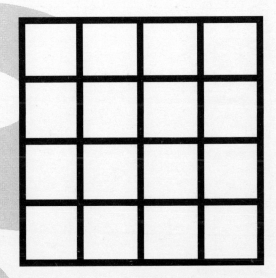

PUZZLE 58

How many squares
of any size can
you find in
this diagram?

? ANSWER NO.3 ?

37

Scales 1 and 2 are in perfect balance.
How many A's are needed to balance the third set?

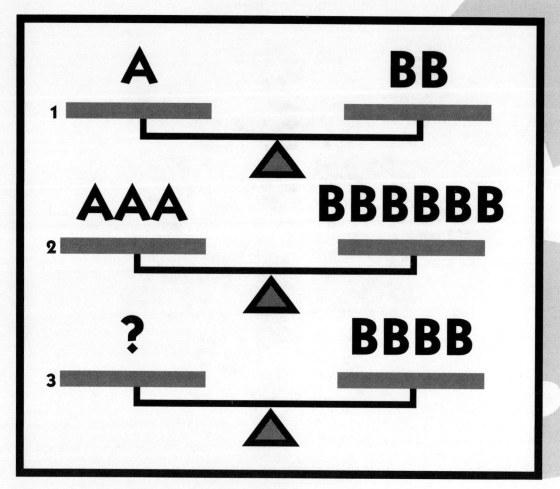

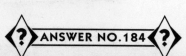

ANSWER NO.123

PUZZLE 60

Divide up the box
into four identical
shapes. The numbers
in each shape add
up to the same.
How is this done?

7	3	3	7
6	4	6	4
3	6	3	7
4	7	6	4

ANSWER NO.184

PUZZLE 61

Which squares contain the same numbers?

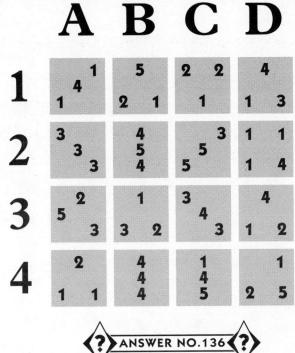

ANSWER NO.136

PUZZLE 62

Which buttons must be used to produce the number on the calculator?

Only three buttons can be used.

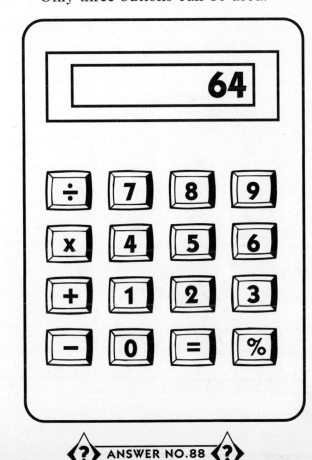

ANSWER NO.88

PUZZLE 63

Fill in the empty boxes so that every line adds up to 10, including the lines that go from corner to corner, using only one number. What is it?

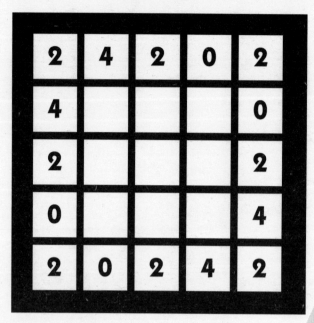

◆? ANSWER NO.63 ?◆

PUZZLE 64

Copy the cake slices out carefully and rearrange them to find the birthday. How old was the birthday girl?

◆? ANSWER NO.170 ?◆

PUZZLE 65

Which of these pictures is not of the same box?

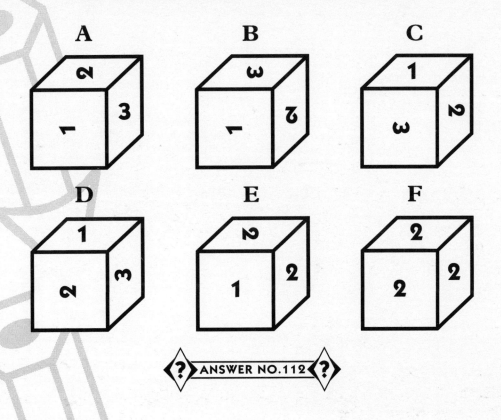

A   B   C

D   E   F

? ANSWER NO.112 ?

PUZZLE 66

Fill up this square with the numbers 1 to 5 so that no row, column
or diagonal line of five squares uses the same number more than once.
What number should replace the question mark?

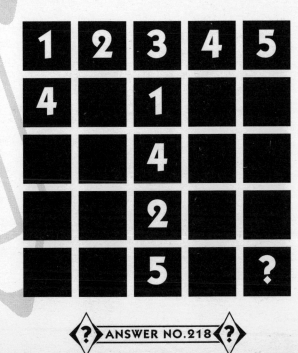

? ANSWER NO.218 ?

41

GETTING HARDER

B

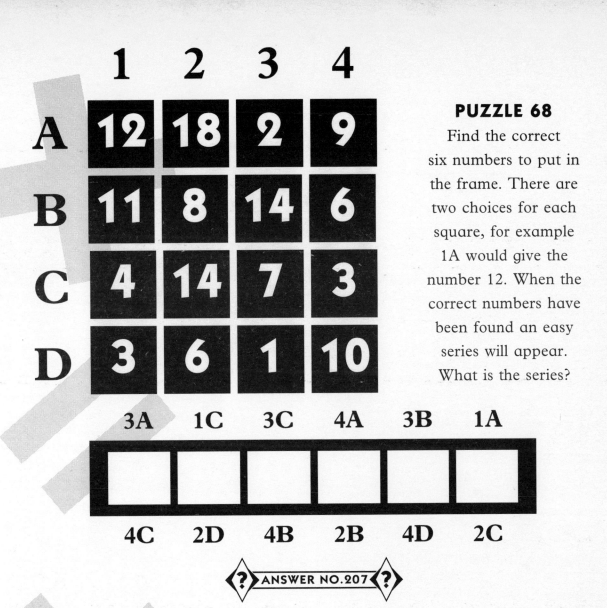

	1	2	3	4
A	12	18	2	9
B	11	8	14	6
C	4	14	7	3
D	3	6	1	10

PUZZLE 68

Find the correct six numbers to put in the frame. There are two choices for each square, for example 1A would give the number 12. When the correct numbers have been found an easy series will appear. What is the series?

3A	1C	3C	4A	3B	1A
4C	2D	4B	2B	4D	2C

◇?◇ ANSWER NO.207 ◇?◇

PUZZLE 69

Which of the numbers in the square is the odd one out and why?

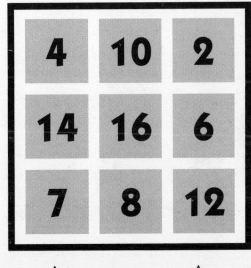

4	10	2
14	16	6
7	8	12

◇?◇ ANSWER NO.52 ◇?◇

PUZZLE 70

Join together the dots using odd numbers only.
Start at the lowest and discover the object. What is it?

15

23 17

2

14

13

19

25

11 21

18

30

B

PUZZLE 71

Using the numbers
shown how many
different ways are
there to add three
numbers together to
make a total of 10?
A number can be
used more than once,
but a group cannot
be repeated in a
different order?

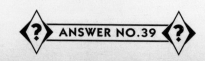

FIENDISH FIGURES

★ LEVEL C ★

PUZZLE 72

The numbers in the middle section have some connection with those down the sides.
Find out what it is and tell us what should replace the question mark?

ANSWER NO.6

45

PUZZLE 73

Move up or across from the bottom left-hand 3 to the top right-hand 3.
Collect nine numbers and add them together. What is the lowest you can score?

<ANSWER NO.175>

PUZZLE 74

Start at any corner and follow the lines. Add up the first four numbers you meet
and then add on the corner number. What is the highest you can score?

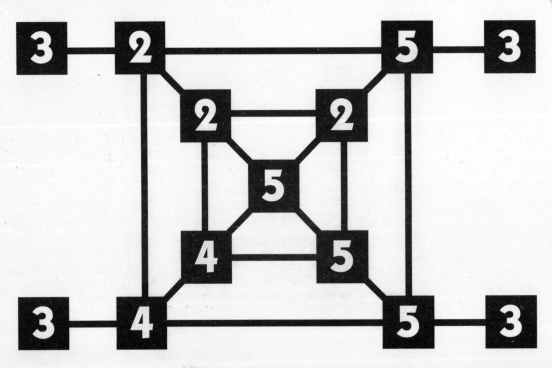

ANSWER NO.53

PUZZLE 75

Place in the middle box a number larger than 1.
If the number is the correct one, all the other numbers can be divided
by it without leaving any remainder. What is the number?

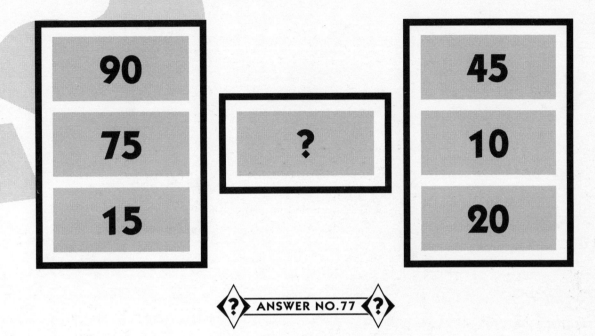

? ANSWER NO.77 ?

PUZZLE 76

Each sector of the circle follows a pattern.
What number should replace the question mark?

? ANSWER NO.149 ?

PUZZLE 77

Copy out these shapes carefully and rearrange them to form a number.
What is it?

 ANSWER NO. 198

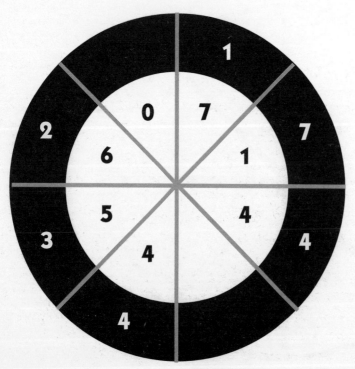

PUZZLE 78

Each slice of this cake adds up to the same number. All the numbers going round the cake total 32. Which numbers should appear in the blanks?

 ANSWER NO. 17

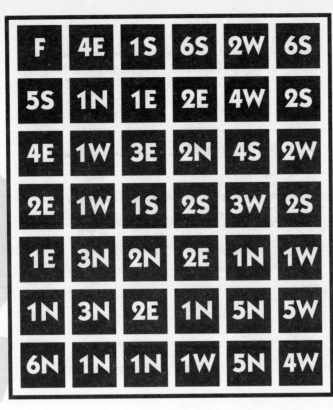

F	4E	1S	6S	2W	6S
5S	1N	1E	2E	4W	2S
4E	1W	3E	2N	4S	2W
2E	1W	1S	2S	3W	2S
1E	3N	2N	2E	1N	1W
1N	3N	2E	1N	5N	5W
6N	1N	1N	1W	5N	4W

PUZZLE 79

Here is an unusual safe. Each of the buttons must be pressed only once in the correct order to open it. The last button is marked F. The number of moves and the direction is marked on each button. Thus 1N would mean one move north, whilst 1W would mean one move to the west. Which button is the first you must press? Here's a clue: it can be found on the middle row.

ANSWER NO.30

PUZZLE 80

If you look carefully you should see why the numbers are written as they are. What number should replace the question mark?

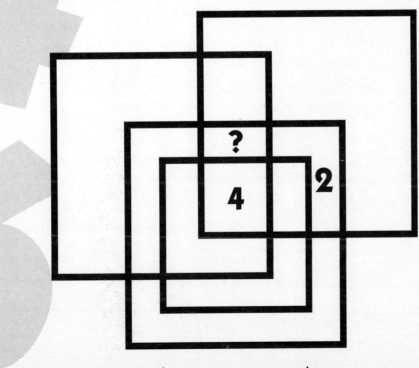

ANSWER NO.18

PUZZLE 81

Look at each line of numbers in the diagram.
What number should replace the question mark?

<?> ANSWER NO.161 <?>

PUZZLE 82

Start at the A and move to B passing through the various parts of the horse.
There is a number in each part and these must be added together.
What is the lowest number you can total?

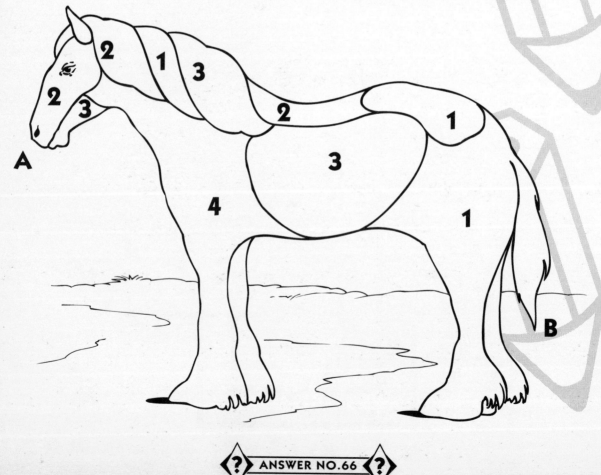

<?> ANSWER NO.66 <?>

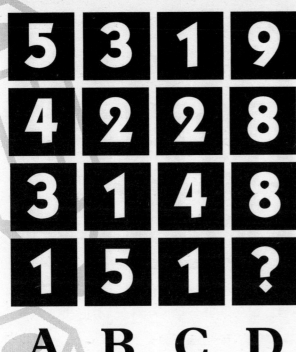

PUZZLE 83

The numbers in column D are linked in some way to those in A, B and C. What number should replace the question mark?

A B C D

ANSWER NO.137

PUZZLE 84

Move from the bottom left-hand 4 to the top right-hand 3 adding together all five numbers. Each black circle is worth minus 1 and this should be taken away from your total each time you meet one. What is the highest total you can find?

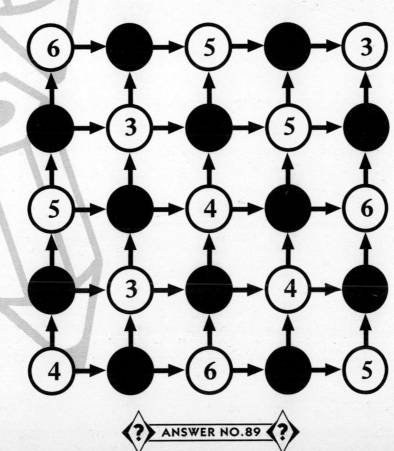

ANSWER NO.89

PUZZLE 85

Each symbol is worth a number. The total of the symbols can be found alongside each row and column. What number should replace the question mark?

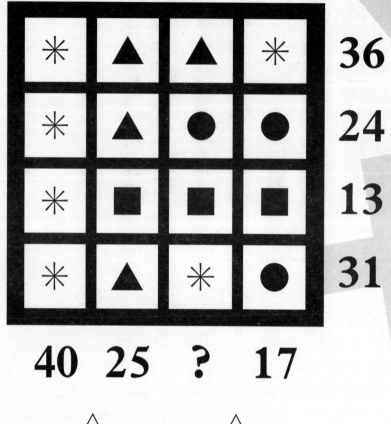

<?> ANSWER NO.185 <?>

PUZZLE 86

On the planet Venox the coins used are 1V, 2V, 5V, 10V, 20V and 50V. A Venoxian has 306V in his squiggly bank. He has the same number of four kinds of coin. How many of each are there and what are they?

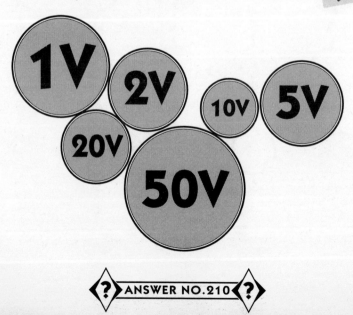

<?> ANSWER NO.210 <?>

PUZZLE 87

What is the lowest number of lines needed to divide the rhinoceros so that you can find the numbers 1, 2, 3, 4 and 5 in each section?

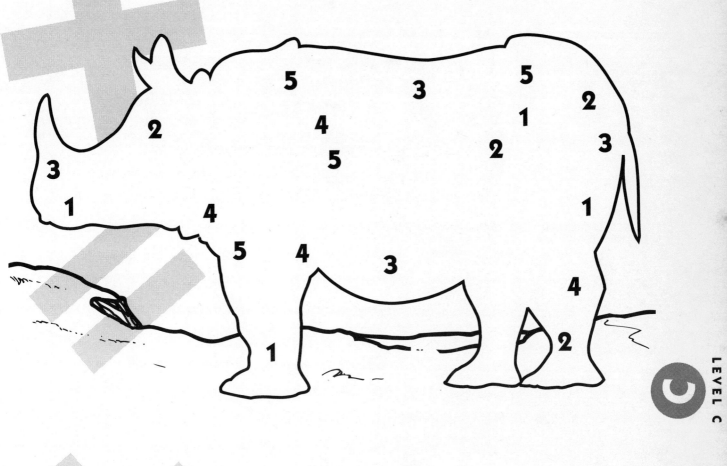

?◆ANSWER NO.102◆?

PUZZLE 88

Replace each question mark with either plus, minus, multiply or divide. Each sign can be used more than once. When the correct ones have been used the sum will be completed. What are the signs?

| 6 | ? | 3 | ? | 4 | ? | 2 | | = | 8 |

?◆ANSWER NO.101◆?

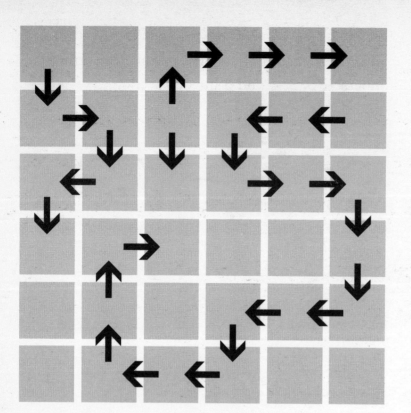

PUZZLE 89

Follow the arrows and find the longest possible route. How many boxes have been entered?

ANSWER NO.113

PUZZLE 90

The symbol on the flag will give a number. What is it?

ANSWER NO.150

PUZZLE 91

Start at the middle 2 and move from circle to touching circle.
Collect three numbers and add them to the 2.
How many different routes are there to make a total of 12?

 **ANSWER NO.29**

PUZZLE 92

Divide up the box
using four lines so
that each shape adds
up to the same.
How is this done?

 **ANSWER NO.186**

55

PUZZLE 93

Scales 1 and 2 are in perfect balance. If one C is the same as four As, how many As are needed to balance the third set?

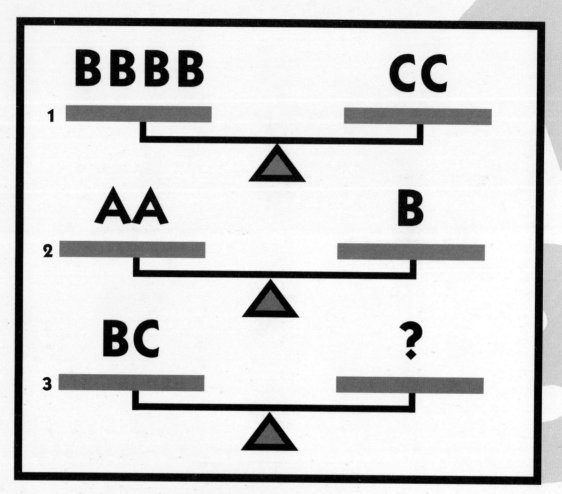

ANSWER NO.125

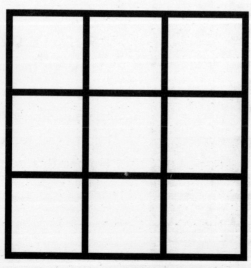

PUZZLE 94

How many rectangles
of any size can
you find in
this diagram?
Remember a square
is also a rectangle!

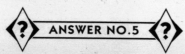
ANSWER NO.5

56

PUZZLE 95

Which squares contain the same numbers?

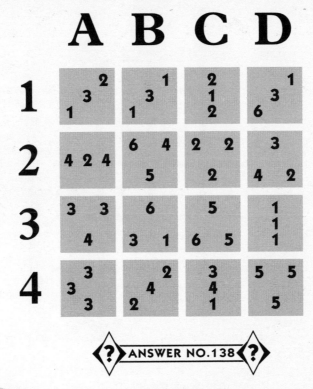

ANSWER NO. 138

PUZZLE 96

One two-digit number should be used to divide the one shown on the calculator to get the answer 11. What is the number?

ANSWER NO. 90

PUZZLE 97

Fill in the empty boxes so that every line adds up to the same, including the lines that go from corner to corner. Which two numbers will be used to do this?

ANSWER NO.65

PUZZLE 98

Copy the cake slices out carefully and rearrange them to find the birthday. How old was the birthday boy?

ANSWER NO.174

58

PUZZLE 99

Which number should replace the question mark to continue the series?

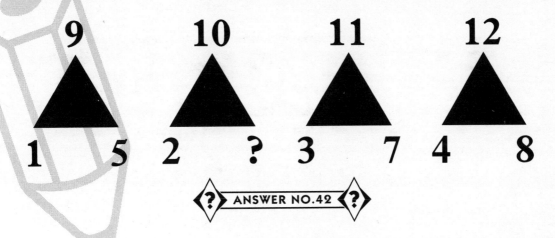

9   10   11   12

1   5   2   ?   3   7   4   8

ANSWER NO.42

PUZZLE 100

Zap the spaceship by finding a one-didgit number which will divide without remainder all the numbers which appear on it. Which number ought you to use?

LEVEL C

ANSWER NO.78

PUZZLE 101

Here is a series of numbers.
Which number should replace the question mark?

◇?◇ ANSWER NO.197 ◇?◇

PUZZLE 102

How many 4s can be found in this stegosaurus?

◇?◇ ANSWER NO.162 ◇?◇

FIENDISH FIGURES

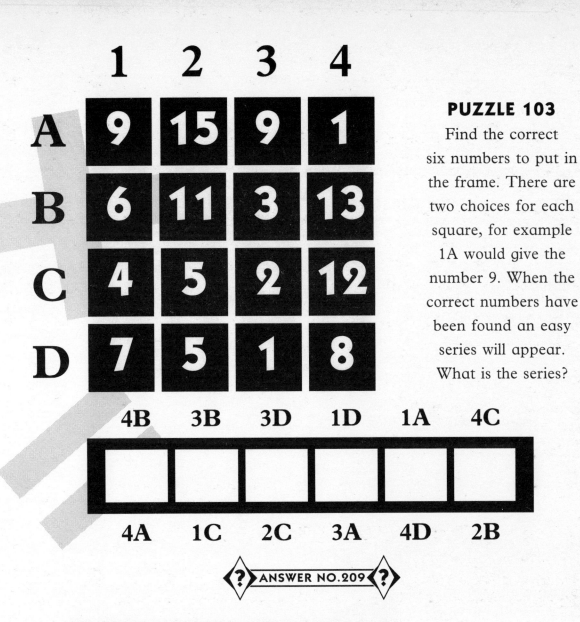

	1	2	3	4
A	9	15	9	1
B	6	11	3	13
C	4	5	2	12
D	7	5	1	8

PUZZLE 103

Find the correct six numbers to put in the frame. There are two choices for each square, for example 1A would give the number 9. When the correct numbers have been found an easy series will appear. What is the series?

4B	3B	3D	1D	1A	4C
4A	1C	2C	3A	4D	2B

ANSWER NO.209

41	7	33	13
21	27	32	63
9	49	3	25
17	29	57	1

PUZZLE 104

Which of the numbers in the square is the odd one out and why?

ANSWER NO.54

PUZZLE 105

Join together the dots using even numbers only.
Start at the lowest and discover the object. What is it?

◆ **?** ◆ ANSWER NO.126 ◆ **?** ◆

PUZZLE 106

Each slice of this cake has a number written on it. Using the numbers shown how many different ways are there to add three numbers together to make a total of 13? A number can be used more than once, but a group cannot be repeated in a different order.

◆ **?** ◆ ANSWER NO.41 ◆ **?** ◆

62

PUZZLE 107

Which of these pictures is not of the same box?

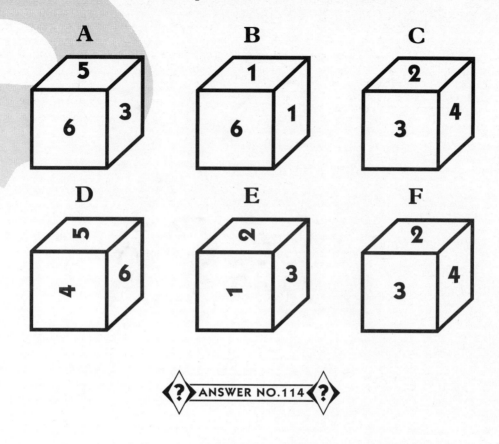

ANSWER NO.114

PUZZLE 108

Fill up this square with the numbers 1 to 5 so that no row, column or diagonal line of five squares uses the same number more than once. What number should replace the question mark?

 ANSWER NO.219

PUZZLE 109

Move up or across from the bottom left-hand 5 to the top right-hand 5.
Collect nine numbers and add them together. What is the highest you can score?

◇?◇ ANSWER NO.49 ◇?◇

MIND NUMBING

★ LEVEL D ★

PUZZLE 110

The numbers in the middle section have some connection with those down the sides.
Find out what it is and tell us what should replace the question mark?

8	4	4
3	1	2
7	2	5
6	5	1
9	?	3

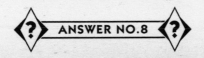
ANSWER NO.8

65

PUZZLE 111

Move up or across from the bottom left-hand 2 to the top right-hand 3.
Collect nine numbers and add them together. What is the highest you can score?

<?> ANSWER NO.173 <?>

PUZZLE 112

Start at any corner and follow the lines. Add up the first four numbers you meet
and then add on the corner number. What is the highest you can score?

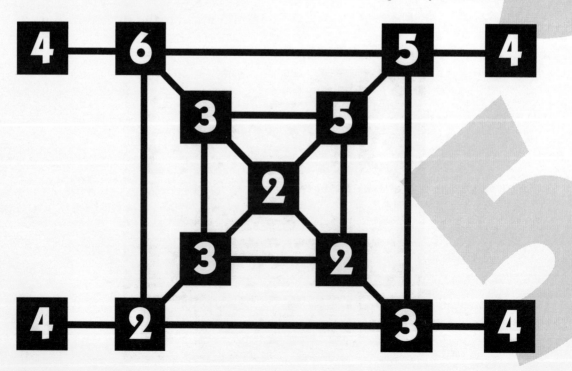

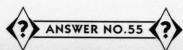

<?> ANSWER NO.55 <?>

PUZZLE 113

Place in the middle box a number larger than 1.
If the number is the correct one, all the other numbers can be divided
by it without leaving any remainder. What is the number?

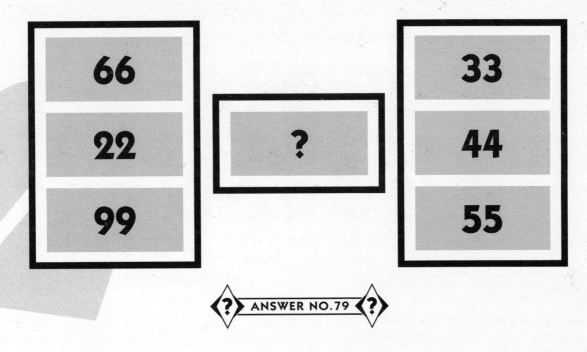

ANSWER NO.79

PUZZLE 114

Each sector of the circle follows a pattern.
What number should replace the question mark?

ANSWER NO.151

LEVEL D

PUZZLE 115

Here is an unusual safe. Each of the buttons must be pressed only once in the correct order to open it. The last button is marked F. The number of moves and the direction is marked on each button. Thus 1i would mean one move in, whilst 1O would mean one move out. 1C would mean one move clockwise and 1A would mean one move anti-clockwise. Which button is the first you must press? Here's a clue: look around the outer rim.

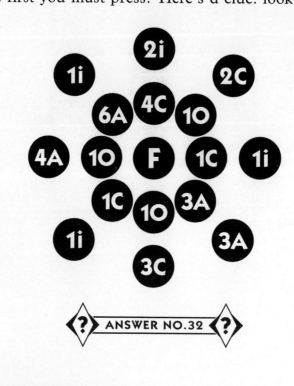

? ANSWER NO.32 **?**

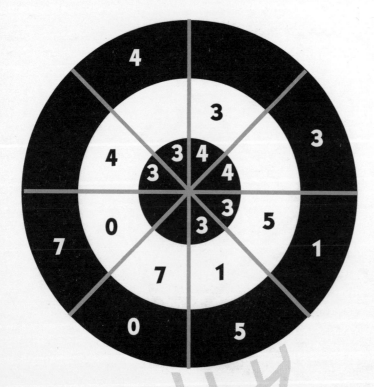

PUZZLE 116

Each slice of this cake adds up to the same number. Also each ring of the cake totals the same. Which number should appear in the blanks?

? ANSWER NO.19 **?**

PUZZLE 117

Copy the cake slices out carefully and rearrange them to find the birthday.
How old was the birthday boy?

? ANSWER NO.176 ?

PUZZLE 118

If you look carefully you should see why the numbers are written as they are.
What number should replace the question mark?

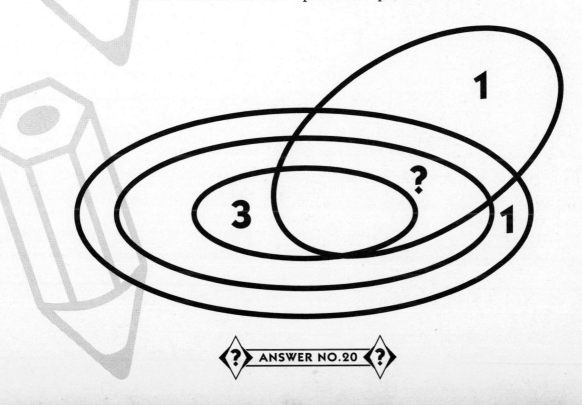

? ANSWER NO.20 ?

PUZZLE 119

Start at the A and move to B passing through various parts of the elephant.
There is a number in each part and these must be added together.
What is the lowest number you can total?

◆❰?❱ ANSWER NO.68 ❰?❱◆

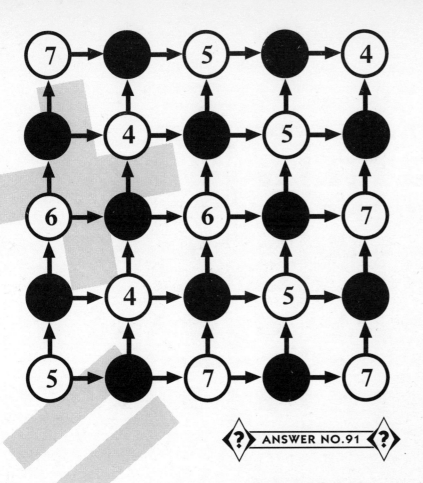

PUZZLE 120

Move from the bottom left-hand 5 to the top right-hand 4 adding together all five numbers. Each black circle is worth minus 3 and this should be taken away from your total each time you meet one. What is the highest total you can find?

? ANSWER NO.91 ?

PUZZLE 121

The numbers in column D are linked in some way to those in A, B and C. What number should replace the question mark?

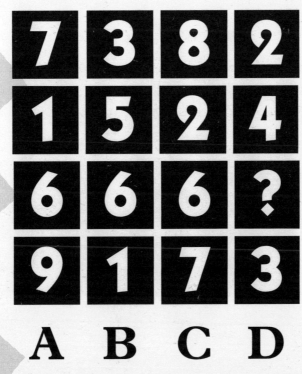

A	B	C	D
7	3	8	2
1	5	2	4
6	6	6	?
9	1	7	3

A B C D

? ANSWER NO.139 ?

PUZZLE 122

Each symbol is worth a number. The total of the symbols can be found alongside each row and column. What number should replace the question mark?

⟨?⟩ ANSWER NO.187 ⟨?⟩

PUZZLE 123

On the planet Venox the coins used are 1V, 2V, 5V, 10V, 20V and 50V.
A Venoxian has 558V in his squiggly bank. He has the same number of four kinds of coin.
How many of each are there and what are they?

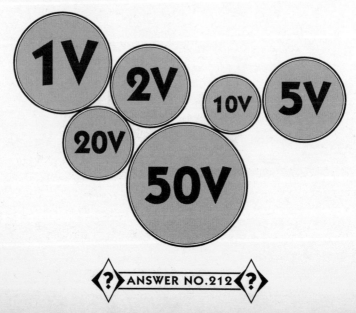

⟨?⟩ ANSWER NO.212 ⟨?⟩

MIND NUMBING

PUZZLE 124

What is the lowest number of lines needed to divide the reindeer so that you can find the numbers 1, 2, 3, 4 and 5 in each section?

◆?◆ ANSWER NO.104 ◆?◆

PUZZLE 125

Replace each question mark with either plus, minus, multiply or divide. Each sign can be used more than once. When the correct ones have been used the sum will be completed. What are the signs?

3 ? 4 ? 3 ? 8 = 7

◆?◆ ANSWER NO.103 ◆?◆

73

PUZZLE 126

Follow the arrows and find the longest possible route.
How many boxes have been entered?

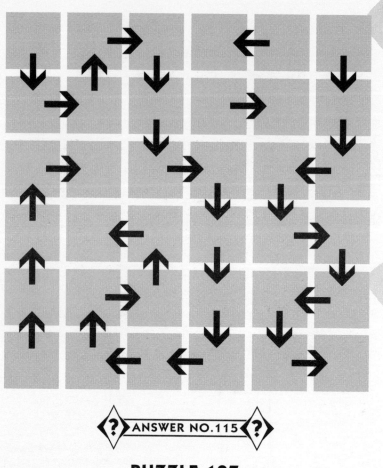

◆ **?** ANSWER NO.115 **?** ◆

PUZZLE 127

The symbol on the flag will give a number. What is it?

◆ **?** ANSWER NO.152 **?** ◆

74

PUZZLE 128

Start at the middle 7 and move from circle to touching circle.
Collect three numbers and add them to the 7.
How many different routes are there to make a total of 20?

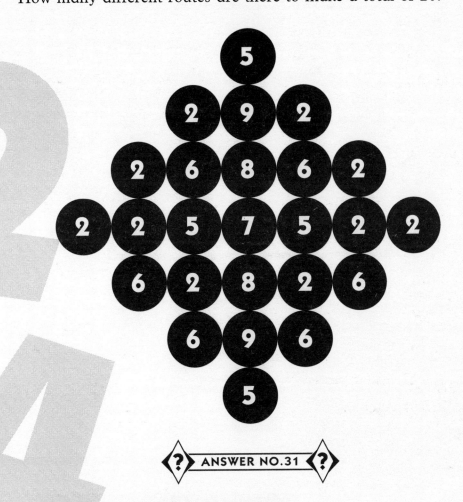

? ANSWER NO.31 ?

PUZZLE 129

Divide up the box
into four identical
shapes. The numbers
in each shape add
up to the same.
How is this done?

? ANSWER NO.188 ?

LEVEL D

PUZZLE 130

Scales 1 and 2 are in perfect balance. If one C is the same as four As, how many As are needed to balance the third set?

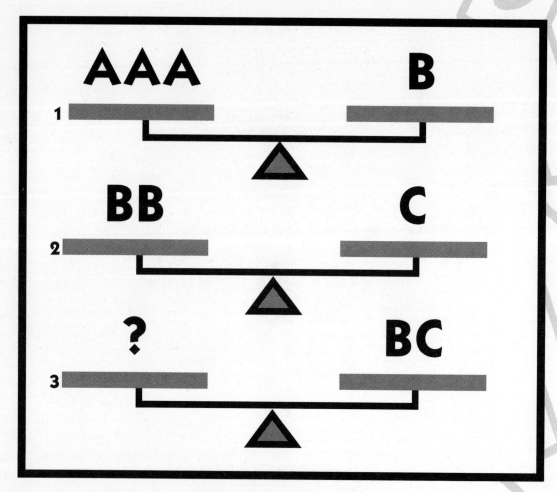

ANSWER NO.127

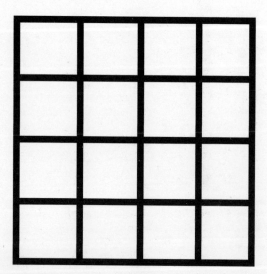

PUZZLE 131

How many rectangles of any size can you find in this diagram?

ANSWER NO.7

MIND NUMBING

A B C D

	A	B	C	D
1	9 4 3	8 7 6	3 8 4	8 2 3
2	1 2 7	9 6 5	9 2 5	5 8 6
3	5 7 8	5 9 2	4 7 2	8 7 9
4	5 2 9	9 8 1	4 9 2	3 1 8

PUZZLE 132

Which squares contain the same numbers?

◆?◆ ANSWER NO.140 ◆?◆

PUZZLE 133

Use either add, subtract, multiply or divide to give the number shown on the calculator. The same number must be used twice. what is the number?

◆?◆ ANSWER NO.92 ◆?◆

LEVEL D

PUZZLE 134

Fill in the empty boxes so that every line adds up to 20.
What number should replace the question mark?

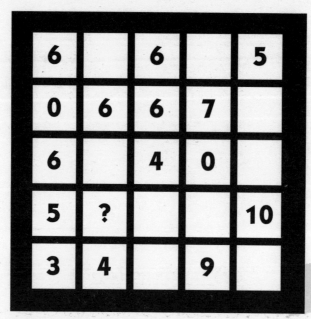

ANSWER NO.67

PUZZLE 135

Copy out these shapes carefully and rearrange them to form a number. What is it?

ANSWER NO.200

PUZZLE 136

Which number should replace the question mark to continue the series?

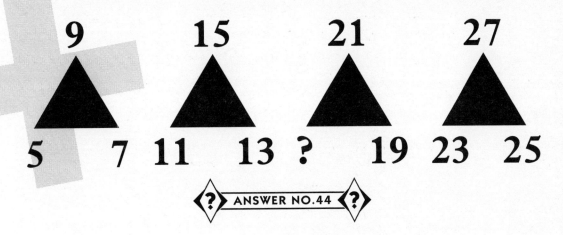

9   15   21   27

5   7   11   13   ?   19   23   25

? ANSWER NO.44 **?**

PUZZLE 137

The number 110 zaps this spaceship. Add together the numbers found on it and multiply the total by either 2, 3, 4, 5, 6, or 7. Which number ought you to use?

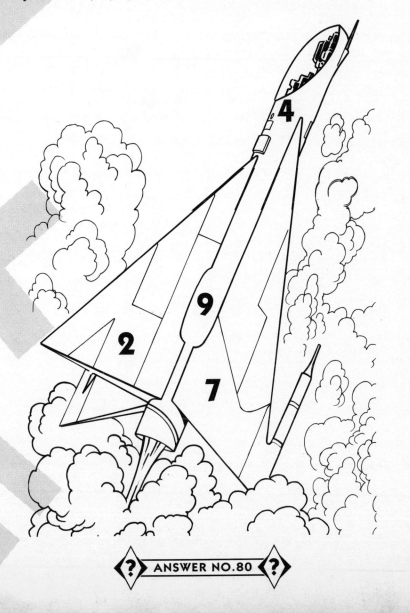

LEVEL D

? ANSWER NO.80 **?**

How many 9's can be found in this Tyrannosaurus Rex?

MIND NUMBING

D

	1	2	3	4
A	2	1	7	21
B	15	17	6	18
C	1	4	11	10
D	3	4	17	19

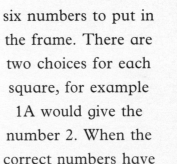

PUZZLE 139

Find the correct six numbers to put in the frame. There are two choices for each square, for example 1A would give the number 2. When the correct numbers have been found an easy series will appear. What is the series?

2A	4B	3B	4C	3A	4A
3D	1D	1A	2D	1B	2C

? ANSWER NO.211 **?**

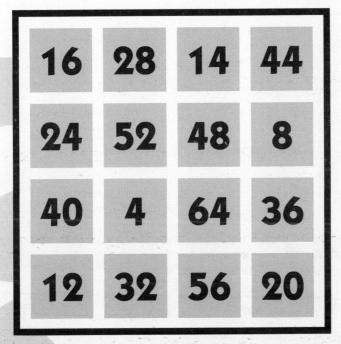

16	28	14	44
24	52	48	8
40	4	64	36
12	32	56	20

PUZZLE 140

Which of the numbers in the square is the odd one out and why?

? ANSWER NO.56 **?**

PUZZLE 141

Join together the dots using only those numbers that can be divided by 10.
Start at the lowest and discover the object. What is it?

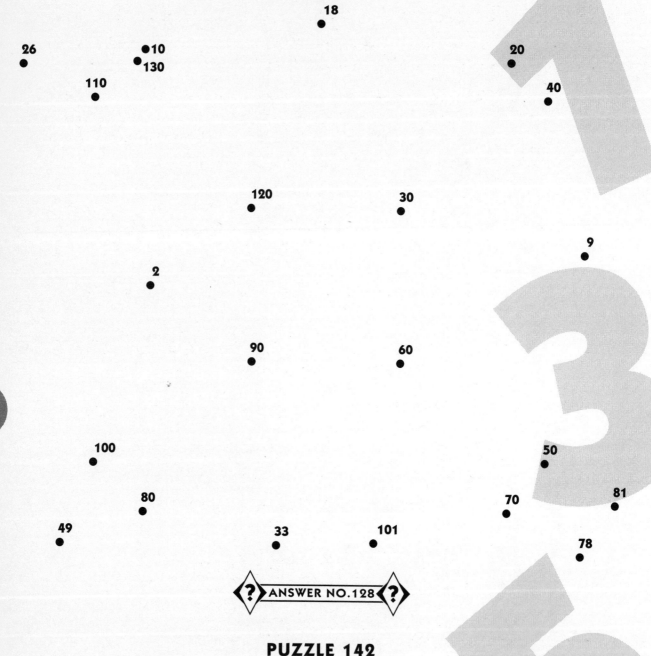

18

26

●10
130

110

20

40

120

30

9

2

90

60

D

100

50

80

70

81

49

33

101

78

◆?◆ ANSWER NO.128 ◆?◆

PUZZLE 142

Here is a series of numbers.
Which number should replace the question mark?

| ? | 128 | 64 | 32 | 16 | 8 | 4 |

◆?◆ ANSWER NO.199 ◆?◆

PUZZLE 143

Which of these pictures is not of the same box?

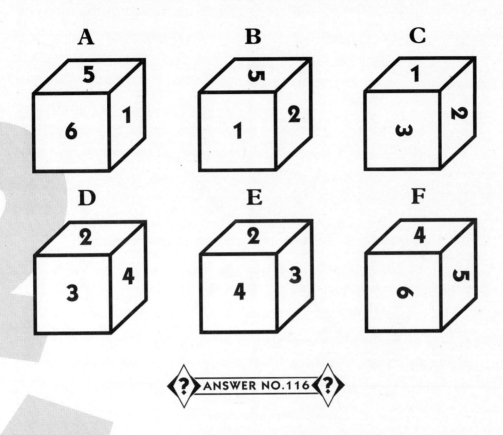

ANSWER NO.116

PUZZLE 144

Fill up this square with the numbers 1 to 5 so that no row, column
or diagonal line of five squares uses the same number more than once.
What number should replace the question mark?

ANSWER NO.74

PUZZLE 145

Each slice of this cake has a number written on it. Using the numbers shown how many different ways are there to add four numbers together to make a total of 12? A number can be used more than once, but a group cannot be repeated in a different order.

? ANSWER NO.43 ?

PUZZLE 146

Look at the pattern of numbers in the diagram.
What number should replace the question mark?

? ANSWER NO.163 ?

AAARGH!

★ LEVEL E ★

PUZZLE 147

The numbers in the middle section have some connection with those down the sides.
Find out what it is and tell us what should replace the question mark?

8	2	4
6	3	2
9	3	3
7	7	1
4	?	2

ANSWER NO.10

PUZZLE 148

Move up or across from the bottom left-hand 8 to the top right-hand 7.
Collect nine numbers and add them together. What is the lowest you can score?

? ANSWER NO.177 ?

AAARGH!

PUZZLE 149

Start at any corner and follow the lines. Add up the first four numbers you meet
and then add on the corner number. How many different routes will add up to 21?

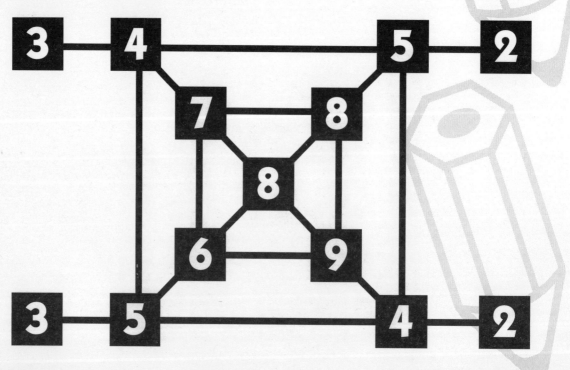

? ANSWER NO.57 ?

PUZZLE 150

Place in the middle box a number larger than 1.
If the number is the correct one, all the other numbers can be divided
by it without leaving any remainder. What is the number?

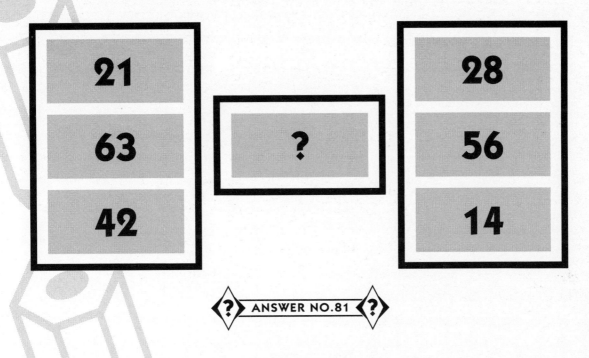

? ANSWER NO.81 **?**

PUZZLE 151

Each sector of the circle follows a pattern.
What number should replace the question mark?

? ANSWER NO.153 **?**

LEVEL E

PUZZLE 152

Here is an unusual safe. Each of the buttons must be pressed only once in the correct order to open it. The last button is marked F. The number of moves and the direction is marked on each button. Thus 1i would mean one move in, whilst 1O would mean one move out. 1C would mean one move clockwise and 1A would mean one move anti-clockwise. Which button is the first you must press? Here's a clue: look on the inner circle.

?◆ ANSWER NO.34 ◆?

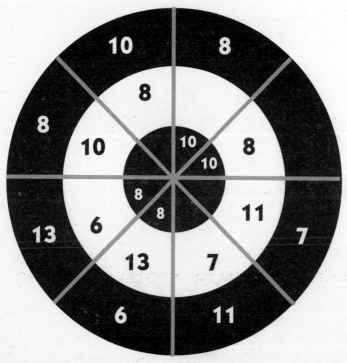

PUZZLE 153

Each slice of this cake adds up to the same number. Also each ring of the cake totals the same. Which number should appear in the blanks?

?◆ ANSWER NO.21 ◆?

PUZZLE 154

Copy the cake slices out carefully and rearrange them to find the birthday.
How old were the twins?

? ANSWER NO.178 **?**

PUZZLE 155

If you look carefully you should see why the numbers are written as they are.
What number should replace the question mark?

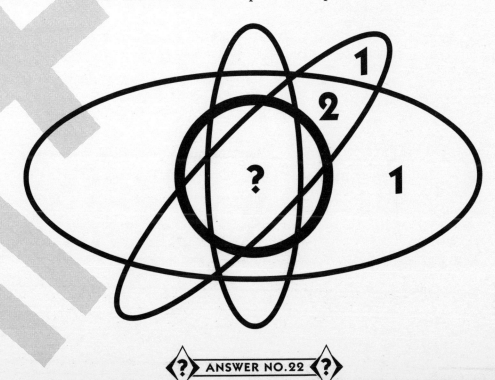

? ANSWER NO.22 **?**

PUZZLE 156

Start at the A and move to B passing through various parts of the cow. There is a number in each part and these must be added together. What is the lowest number you can total?

? ANSWER NO.70 ?

PUZZLE 157

Each sector of this wheel has a number written on it. Using the numbers shown how many different ways are there to add four numbers together to make a total of 14? A number can be used more than once, but a group cannot be repeated in a different order.

? ANSWER NO.45 ?

AAARGH!

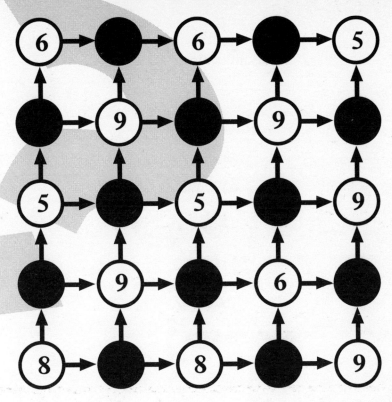

PUZZLE 158

Move from the bottom left-hand 8 to the top right-hand 5 adding together all five numbers. Each black circle is worth minus 4 and this should be taken away from your total each time you meet one. What is the lowest total and how many different routes are there to find it?

ANSWER NO.93

LEVEL E

PUZZLE 159

The numbers in column D are linked in some way to those in A, B and C. What number should replace the question mark?

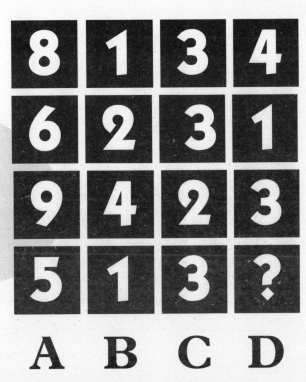

A B C D

ANSWER NO.141

PUZZLE 160

Each symbol is worth a number. The total of the symbols can be found alongside each row and column. What number should replace the question mark?

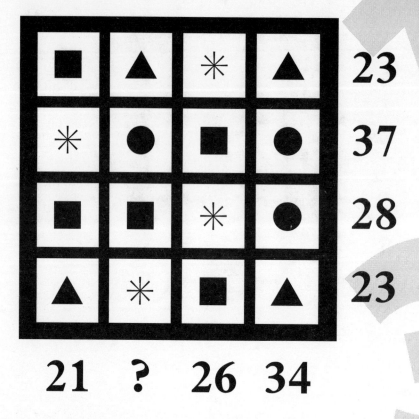

ANSWER NO.189

PUZZLE 161

On the planet Venox the coins used are 1V, 2V, 5V, 10V, 20V and 50V. A Venoxian has 2,349V in his squiggly bank. He has the same number of five kinds of coin. How many of each are there and what are they?

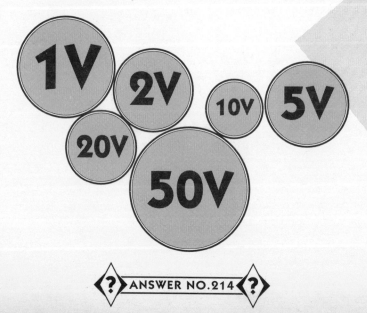

ANSWER NO.214

PUZZLE 162

What is the lowest number of lines needed to divide the bear so that
you can find the numbers 1, 2, 3, 4, 5 and 6 in each section?

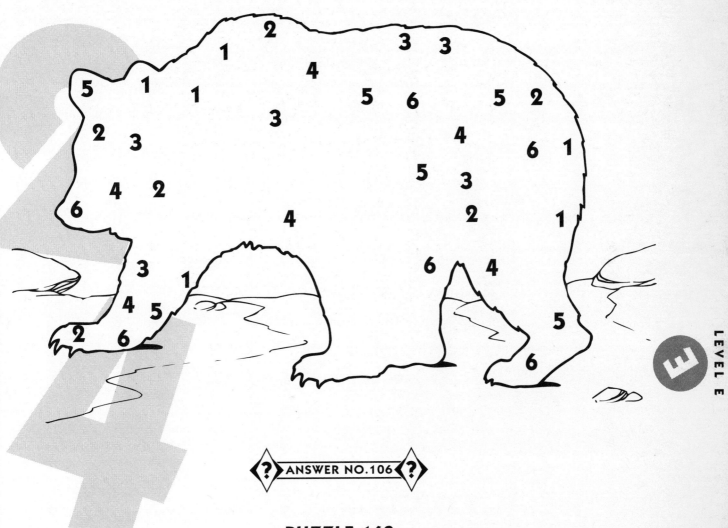

◆?▷ANSWER NO.106◁?◆

PUZZLE 163

Replace each question mark with either plus, minus, multiply or divide.
Each sign can be used more than once. When the correct ones have been used
the sum will be completed. What are the signs?

| 4 | ? | 5 | ? | 3 | ? | 8 | = | 24 |

◆?▷ANSWER NO.105◁?◆

PUZZLE 164

Follow the arrows and find the longest possible route.
How many boxes have been entered?

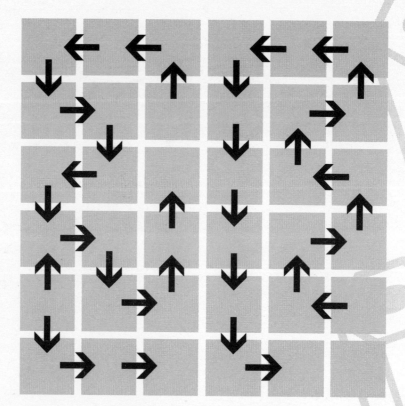

ANSWER NO.117

PUZZLE 165

The symbol on the flag will give a number. What is it?

ANSWER NO.154

94

PUZZLE 166

Start at the middle 5 and move from circle to touching circle.
Collect three numbers and add them to the 5.
How many different routes are there to make a total of 16?

ANSWER NO.33

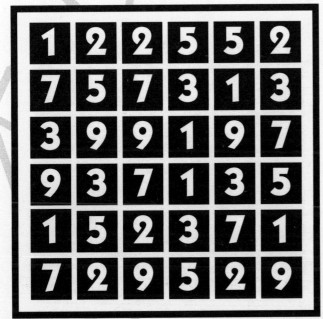

PUZZLE 167

Divide up the box
into six identical
shapes. The numbers
in each shape add
up to the same.
How is this done?

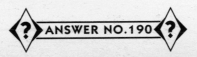

ANSWER NO.190

PUZZLE 168

Scales 1 and 2 are in perfect balance.
How many Cs are needed to balance the third set?

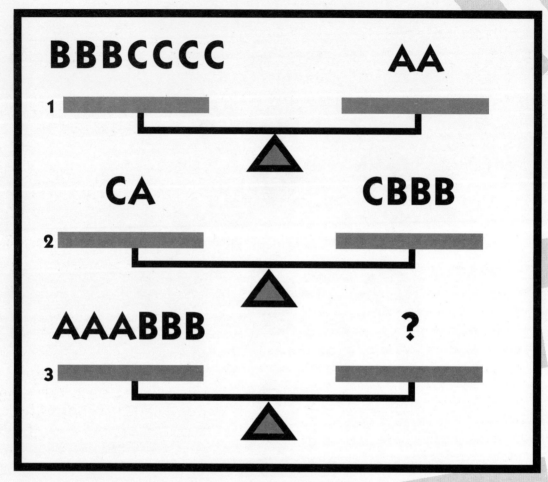

? ANSWER NO.129 **?**

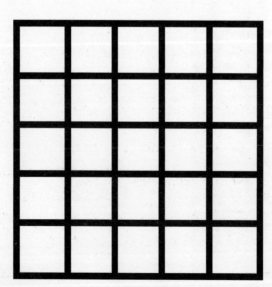

PUZZLE 169

How many squares
of any size can
you find in
this diagram?

? ANSWER NO.9 **?**

96

A B C D E

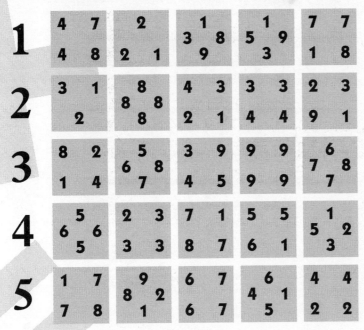

PUZZLE 170

Which squares contain the same numbers?

ANSWER NO.142

PUZZLE 171

What is the least number of buttons you must press to turn the number shown on the calculator into 17?

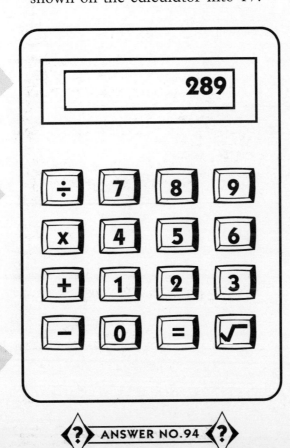

ANSWER NO.94

PUZZLE 172

Fill in the empty boxes, using two numbers only, so that every line adds up to 25.
What number should replace the question mark?

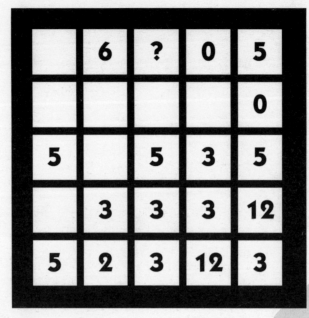

ANSWER NO.69

AAARGH!

PUZZLE 173

Copy out these shapes carefully and rearrange
them to form a number. What is it?

ANSWER NO.202

PUZZLE 174

Which number should replace the question mark to continue the series?

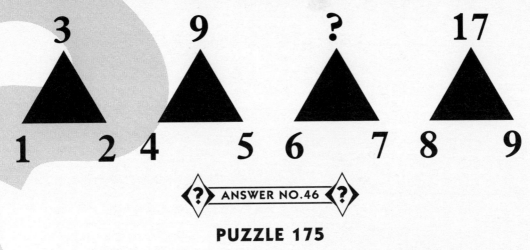

3   9   ?   17

1   2   4   5   6   7   8   9

❮?❯ ANSWER NO.46 ❮?❯

PUZZLE 175

To zap the spaceship find the number which, when multiplied by itself, will equal the total of the numbers shown. What is the number?

❮?❯ ANSWER NO.84 ❮?❯

PUZZLE 176

How many 2's can be found in this Triceratops?

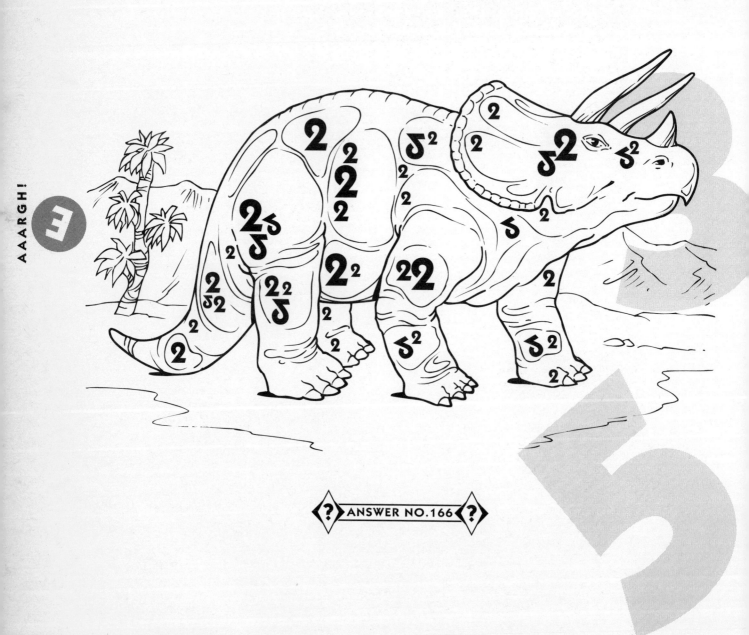

ANSWER NO.166

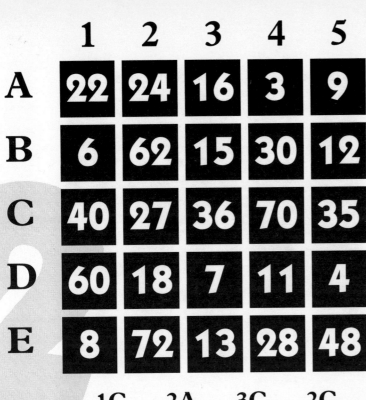

	1	2	3	4	5
A	22	24	16	3	9
B	6	62	15	30	12
C	40	27	36	70	35
D	60	18	7	11	4
E	8	72	13	28	48

PUZZLE 177

Find the correct six numbers to put in the frame. There are two choices for each square, for example 1A would give the number 22. When the correct numbers have been found a series will appear. What is the series?

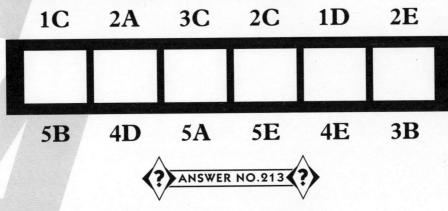

1C	2A	3C	2C	1D	2E
5B	4D	5A	5E	4E	3B

ANSWER NO.213

LEVEL E

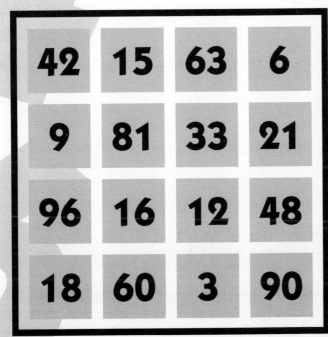

42	15	63	6
9	81	33	21
96	16	12	48
18	60	3	90

PUZZLE 178

Which of the numbers in the square is the odd one out and why?

ANSWER NO.58

PUZZLE 179

Join together the dots using only those numbers that can be divided by 5.
Start at the lowest and discover the object. What is it?

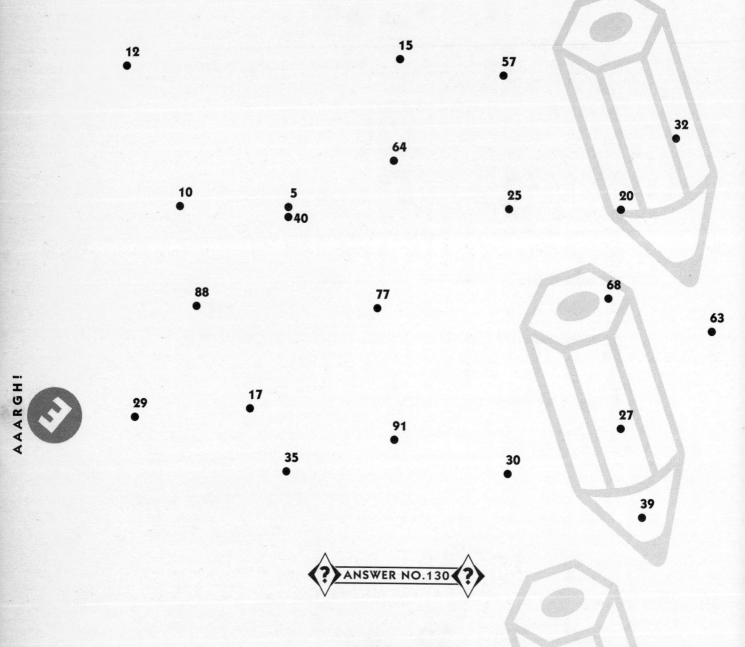

AAARGH!

? ANSWER NO.130 ?

PUZZLE 180

Here is a series of numbers.
Which number should replace the question mark?

| 32 | 25 | ? | 14 | 10 | 7 | 5 |

? ANSWER NO.201 ?

PUZZLE 181

Which of these pictures is not of the same box?

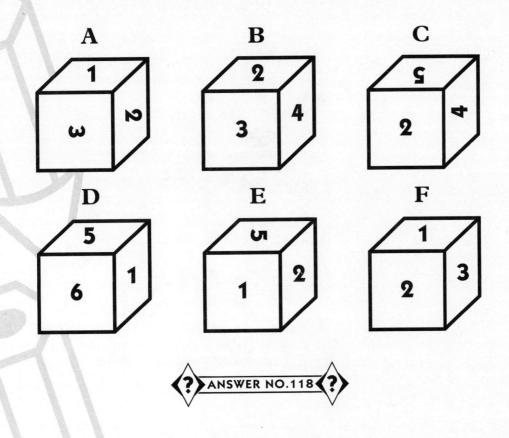

A   B   C

D   E   F

◇?◇ ANSWER NO.118 ◇?◇

PUZZLE 182

Fill up this square with the numbers 1 to 5 so that no row, column or diagonal line of five squares uses the same number more than once. What number should replace the question mark?

◇?◇ ANSWER NO.50 ◇?◇

PUZZLE 183

Look at the pattern of numbers in the diagram.
What number should replace the question mark?

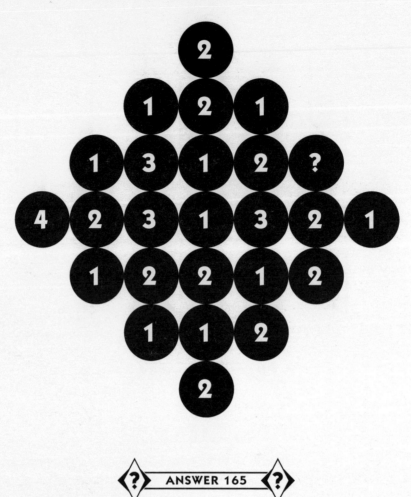

❮?❯ ANSWER 165 ❮?❯

SUPER GENIUS

★ LEVEL F ★

PUZZLE 184

The numbers in the middle section have some connection with those down the sides. Find out what it is and tell us what should replace the question mark?

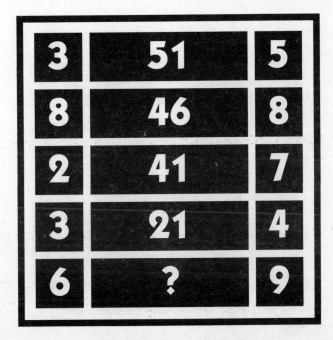

3	51	5
8	46	8
2	41	7
3	21	4
6	?	9

ANSWER NO.12

105

PUZZLE 185

Move up or across from the bottom left-hand 5 to the top right-hand 3.
Collect nine numbers and add them together. What is the highest you can score?

? ANSWER NO.179 **?**

PUZZLE 186

Start at any corner and follow the lines. Add up the first four numbers you meet
and then add on the corner number. What is the lowest possible total
and how many different routes lead to it?

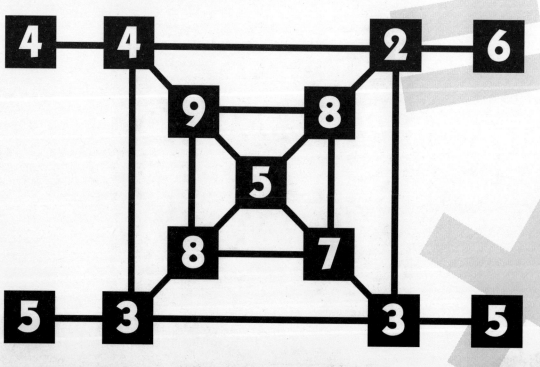

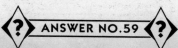**?** ANSWER NO.59 **?**

PUZZLE 187

Place in the middle box a number larger than 1.
If the number is the correct one, all the other numbers can be divided
by it without leaving any remainder. What is the number?

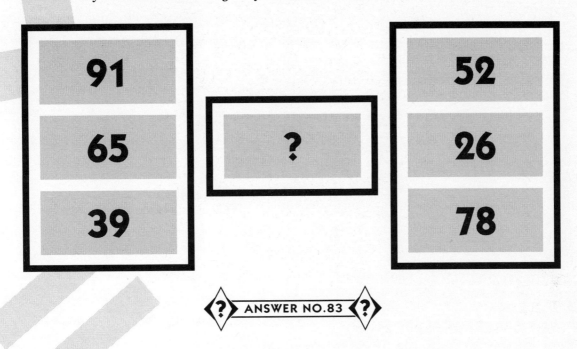

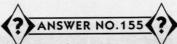 ANSWER NO.83

PUZZLE 188

Each sector of the circle follows a pattern.
What number should replace the question mark?

ANSWER NO.155

PUZZLE 189

Here is an unusual safe. Each of the buttons must be pressed only once in the correct order to open it. The last button is marked F. The number of moves and the direction is marked on each button. Thus 1i would mean one move in, whilst 1O would mean one move out. 1C would mean one move clockwise and 1A would mean one move anti-clockwise. Which button is the first you must press? Here's a clue: look on the outer rim.

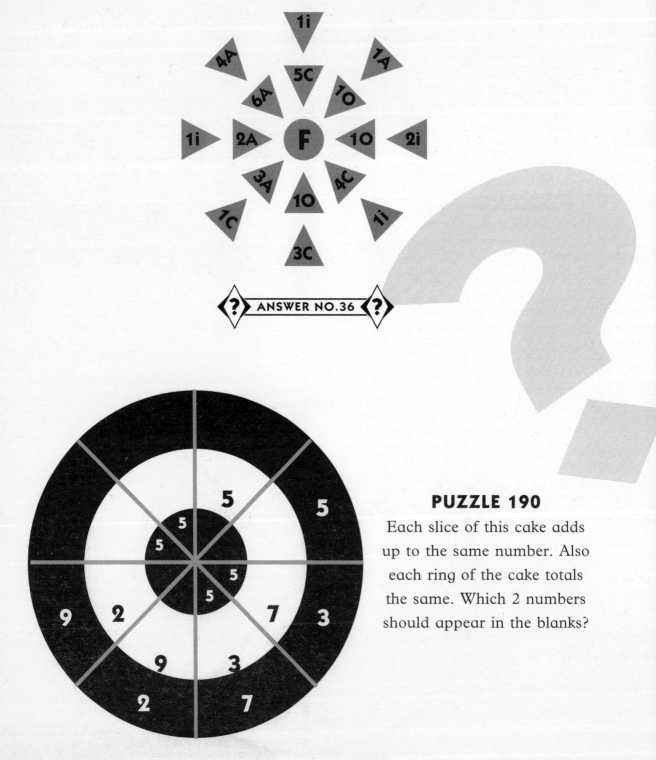

ANSWER NO.36

PUZZLE 190

Each slice of this cake adds up to the same number. Also each ring of the cake totals the same. Which 2 numbers should appear in the blanks?

ANSWER NO.23

PUZZLE 191

Copy the cake slices out carefully and rearrange them to find the birthday.
How old was the birthday girl?

❖? ANSWER NO.180 ?❖

PUZZLE 192

If you look carefully you should see why the numbers are written as they are.
What number should replace the question mark?

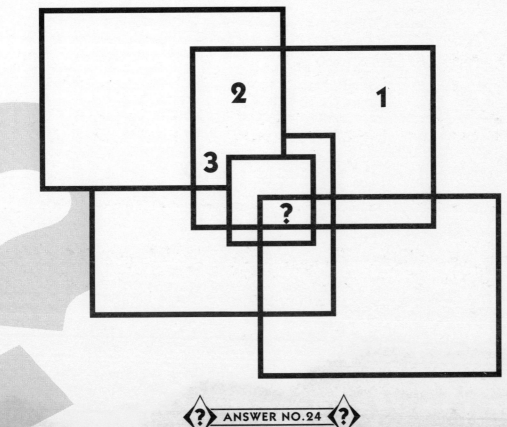

❖? ANSWER NO.24 ?❖

PUZZLE 193

Start at the A and move to B passing through the various parts of the duck.
There is a number in each part and these must be added together.
What is the lowest number you can total?

◇❓ ANSWER NO.72 ❓◇

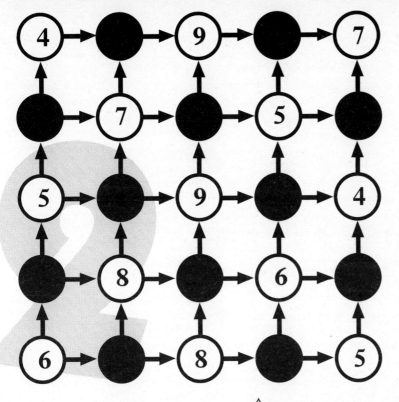

PUZZLE 194

Move from the bottom left-hand 6 to the top right-hand 7 adding together all five numbers. Each black circle is worth minus 5 and this should be taken away from your total each time you meet one.
How many different routes, each giving a total of 10, can be found?

ANSWER NO.95

LEVEL F

PUZZLE 195

The numbers in column D are linked in some way to those in A, B and C. What number should replace the question mark?

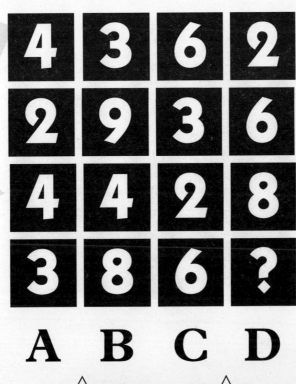

4	3	6	2
2	9	3	6
4	4	2	8
3	8	6	?

A   B   C   D

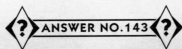
ANSWER NO.143

PUZZLE 196

Each symbol is worth a number. The total of the symbols can be found alongside a row and two columns. What number should replace the question mark?

85

? 50 45

ANSWER NO.191

PUZZLE 197

On the planet Venox the coins used are 1V, 2V, 5V, 10V, 20V and 50V. A Venoxian has 3,071V in his squiggly bank. He has the same number of five kinds of coin. How many of each are there and what are they?

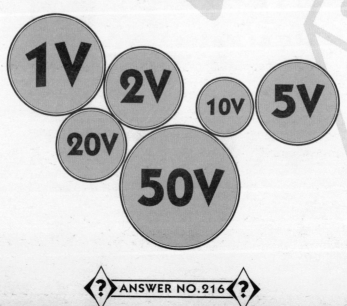

ANSWER NO.216

PUZZLE 198

What is the lowest number of lines needed to divide the cat so that the numbers in each section always total 17?

◆ ? ▸ ANSWER NO.108 ◂ ? ◆

PUZZLE 199

Replace each question mark with either plus, minus, multiply or divide. Each sign can be used more than once. When the correct ones have been used the sum will be completed. What are the signs?

| 10 | ? | 2 | ? | 7 | ? | 3 | = | 32 |

◆ ? ▸ ANSWER NO.107 ◂ ? ◆

LEVEL F

113

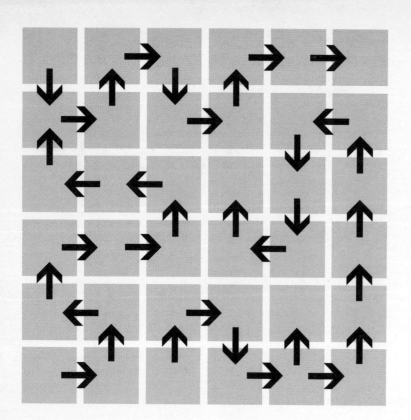

PUZZLE 200

Follow the arrows and find the longest possible route. How many boxes have been entered?

 ANSWER NO.119

PUZZLE 201

The symbol on the flag will give a number. What is it?

 ANSWER NO.156

PUZZLE 202

Start at the middle 9 and move from circle to touching circle. Collect three numbers and add them to the 9. How many different routes are there to make a total of 17?

?ANSWER NO.35?

PUZZLE 203

Divide up the box into four identical shapes. The numbers in each shape add up to the same. How is this done?

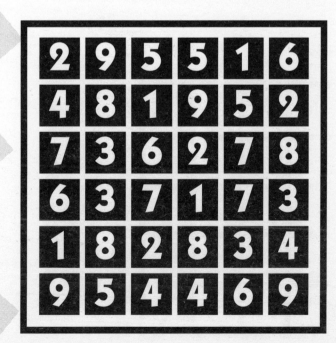

?ANSWER NO.192?

PUZZLE 204

Scales 1 and 2 are in perfect balance.
How many Bs are needed to balance the third set?

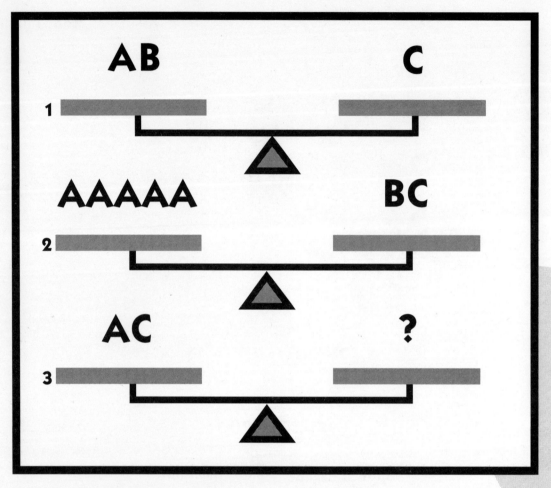

ANSWER NO.131

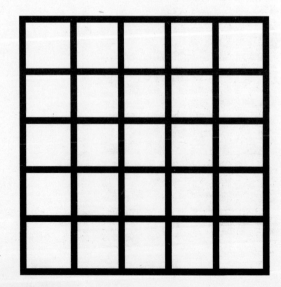

PUZZLE 205

How many rectangles
of any size can
you find in
this diagram?

ANSWER NO.11

PUZZLE 206

Which squares contain the same numbers?

A B C D E

	A	B	C	D	E
1	3 4 / 6 9	1 8 / 3 3 8	2 6 / 4 8	1 2 3 / 2 4	1 6 / 3 9
2	5 / 1 3 / 5	9 / 1 2 / 8	2 / 3 3 / 2	1 / 3 9 / 7	5 / 6 / 5 5
3	1 / 3 / 9 6	1 / 4 7 / 8	4 / 4 3 / 3	6 / 3 9 / 1	1 5 / 9 8
4	7 7 / 6 6	6 7 / 8 / 9	9 / 9 8 / 2	9 9 / 9 / 1	9 6 / 4 8
5	4 / 6 / 3 7	8 / 2 / 3 4	3 1 / 6 9	4 / 4 6 / 9	8 8 / 8 8

ANSWER NO.144

PUZZLE 207

How many ways are there to score 25 on this dartboard using four darts only? Each dart always lands in a segment and no dart falls to the floor. Once a group of numbers has been used it cannot be repeated in a different order.

ANSWER NO.47

117

PUZZLE 208

Fill in the empty boxes so that every line adds up to 30. Use two numbers only, one of which is double the other. What number should replace the question mark?

ANSWER NO. 71

PUZZLE 209

Copy out these shapes carefully and rearrange them to form a number. What is it?

ANSWER NO. 204

PUZZLE 210

Which number should replace the question mark to continue the series?

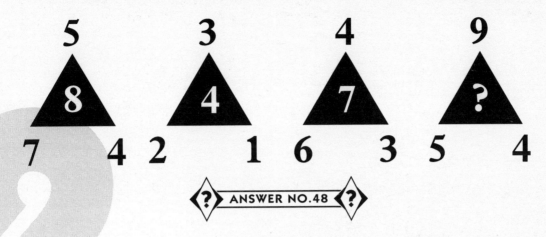

? ANSWER NO.48 ?

PUZZLE 211

To zap the spaceship find the number which, when multiplied by itself, will equal the total of the numbers shown. What is the number?

? ANSWER NO.82 ?

PUZZLE 212

How many 8's can be found in this Brontosaurus?

ANSWER NO. 168

SUPER GENIUS

1 2 3 4

	1	2	3	4
A	7	16	11	4
B	1	12	18	3
C	9	13	8	14
D	5	2	17	2

PUZZLE 213

Find the correct six numbers to put in the frame. There are two choices for each square, for example 1A would give the number 7. When the correct numbers have been found an easy series will appear. What is the series?

4D	2C	4A	1A	3A	3D
1B	4B	1D	3C	1C	2C

◆? ANSWER NO.215 ?◆

3	17	11	9
5	15	7	13
12	8	1	19
2	10	16	4

PUZZLE 214

Which two numbers on the square do not fit the pattern and why?

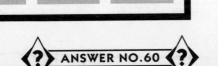

◆? ANSWER NO.60 ?◆

PUZZLE 215

Join together the dots using only those numbers that can be divided by 4.
Start at the lowest and discover the object. What is it?

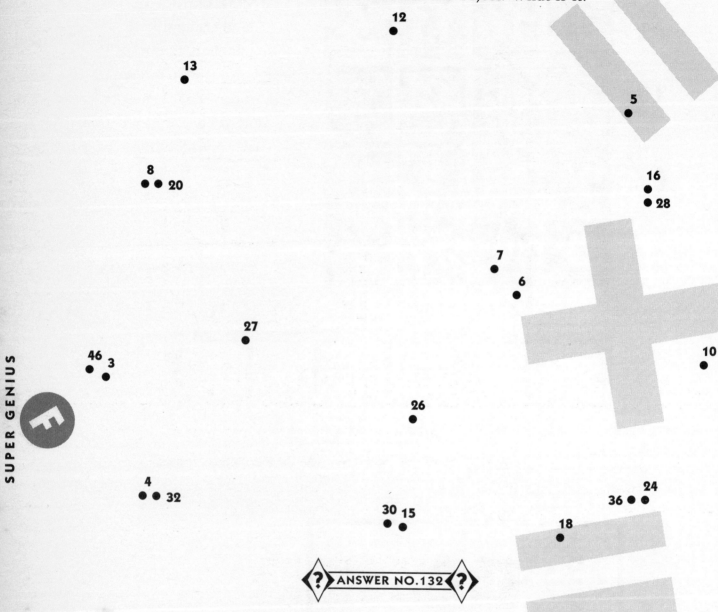

12

13

5

8 20

16
28

7
6

27

46 3

10

26

4 32

24
36

30 15

18

◆?◆ ANSWER NO.132 ◆?◆

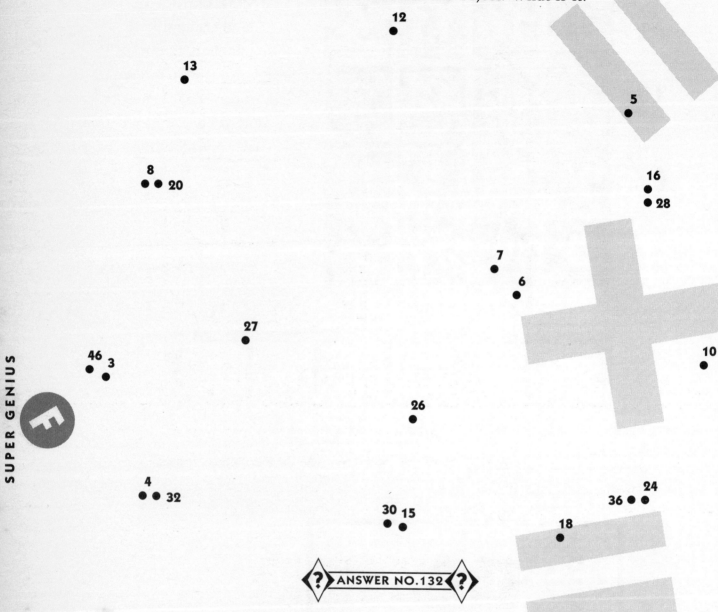

SUPER GENIUS

PUZZLE 216

Here is a series of numbers.
Which number should replace the question mark?

| 49 | 7 | 9 | 3 | 64 | 8 | 25 | ? |

◆?◆ ANSWER NO.203 ◆?◆

122

PUZZLE 217

Which of these pictures are not of the same box?

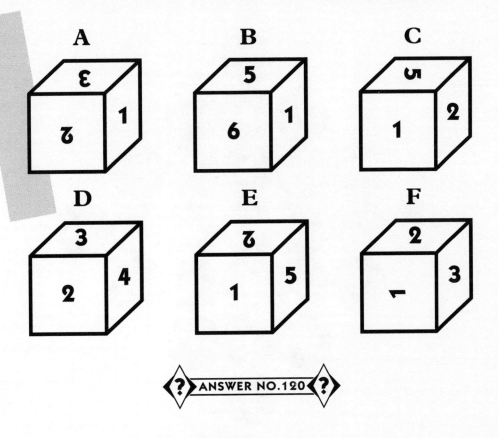

? ANSWER NO.120 ?

PUZZLE 218

Fill up this square with the numbers 1 to 5 so that no row, column
or diagonal line of five squares uses the same number more than once.
What number should replace the question mark?

? ANSWER NO.96 ?

PUZZLE 219

Look at the pattern of number in the diagram.
What number should replace the question mark?

ANSWER NO.167

ANSWERS

1   14.

2   8. The numbers down the sides are placed together in the middle section.

3   30.

4   19. The numbers down the sides are placed together in the middle section in reverse order.

5   36.

6   11. The numbers down the sides are added together to give the number in the middle section.

7   100.

8   6. The number down the right-hand side is taken from the the number down the left-hand side to give the number in the middle section.

9   55.

10   2. The number down the left-hand side is divided by the number down the right-hand side to give the number in the middle section.

11   225.

12   45. The numbers down the sides are multiplied together to give the number in the middle section, placed in a reversed order.

13   3.

14   1. The number is surrounded by only one shape.

15   2 in the outer section and 4 in the inner one.

16   3. The number is found in 3 overlapping shapes.

17   8 in the outer section at the top, 3 in the outer section below and 5 in the inner one.

18   3. The number is found in 3 overlapping shapes.

19   2.

20   3. The number is found in 3 overlapping shapes.

21   9.

22   4. The number is found in 4 overlapping shapes.

23   4 and 6.

24   4. The number is found in 4 overlapping shapes.

25   4.

26   2D, in the third column.

27   7.

28   1R.

29   6.

30   2S, in the fourth column.

31   10.

32   1i, found between 4A and 3C.

33   13.

34   1C.

35   12.

36   1C.

37   9.

38   8.

39   8.

40   9.

41   8.

42   6. Move from triangle to triangle, beginning on the left, to read 1, 2, 3, 4. Start again to get 5, 6, 7, 8. Then move to the top to get 9, 10, 11, 12.

43   7.

44   17. Odd numbers increase in order from left, to right, to top around each triangle.

45   23.

46   13. The two numbers at the base of each triangle are added to give the top number.

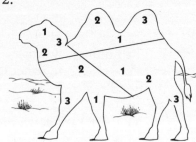

47 22.

48 10. The left-hand number is added to the top number and then the right-hand number is subtracted to give the centre number.

49 42.

50 3.

51 14.

52 7. It is the only odd number.

53 23.

54 32. It is the only even number.

55 23.

56 14. All the other numbers are divisible by 4.

57 4.

58 16. All the other numbers are divisible by 3.

59 16 is the lowest and there are 2 routes.

60 Each pair of numbers on each row total 20. The first two on the bottom row, 2 and 10, do not.

61 1.

62 11.

63 2.

64 12.

65 0 and 6.

66 10.

67 1.

68 27.

69 7.

70 31.

71 4.

72 13.

73 2.

74 4.

75 3.

76 19.

77 5.

78 2.

79 11.

80 5.

81 7.

82 12.

83 13.

84 13.

85 19.

86 Times and 2.

87 30.

88 8, times and 8.

89 20.

90 12.

91 18.

92 2. 2 times 2 or 2 plus 2.

93 13 and one way.

94 1. Square root. ($\sqrt{\ }$)

95 5.

96 3.

97 Plus and plus.

98 2.

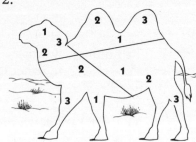

99 Plus and minus.

100 3.

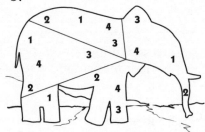

101 Minus, times and plus.

102 3.

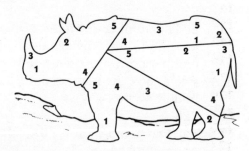

103 Multiply, plus and minus.

104 4.

105 Plus, divide and multiply.

106 4.

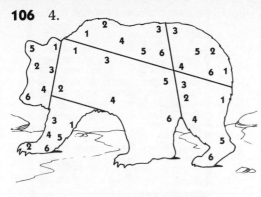

107 Divide, multiply and minus.

108 4.

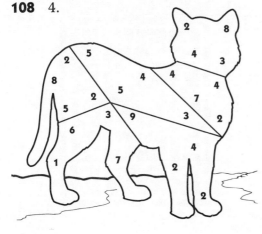

109 18.
110 C.
111 13.
112 F.
113 16.
114 B.
115 17.
116 E.
117 17.
118 F.
119 19.
120 D and E.
121 6.
122 A hammer.
123 2.
124 A tent.
125 6.
126 A Star.
127 9.
128 A Maltese Cross.
129 16.
130 An arrow.
131 2.
132 An envelope.
133 6. Add together A, B and C to get D.

134 1A and 3C.
135 9. Add together A, B and C in order to get D.
136 1B and 4D.
137 7. Add together A, B and C to get D.
138 3B and 1D.
139 6. Add together A and B, then take away C in order to get D.
140 2C, 3B and 4A.
141 1. A minus B minus C gives D.
142 1E, 4C and 5A.
143 4. A times B divided by C gives D.
144 1E, 3A, 3D and 5C.
145 3. Each sector contains the numbers 1, 2 and 3.
146 3. A 3 and its mirror image are placed together.
147 23. The numbers 1 to 24 are contained in the sectors.
148 7. A 7 and its mirror image are placed together.
149 2. The numbers in each sector total 12.
150 4. A 4 and its mirror image are placed together.
151 1. Each sector's total increases by 1.
152 2. A 2 and its mirror image are placed together top and bottom.
153 3. Opposite sectors total the same.
154 3. A 3, on its side, and its mirror image are placed together.
155 9. Each sector in the bottom half of the circle totals double its opposite.
156 5. A 5 and its mirror image are placed together.
157 1. The pattern is symmetrical.
158 10.
159 2. The pattern is symmetrical.
160 26.
161 4. The total of each horizontal line increases by 1.
162 30.
163 9. Each column of numbers totals 9.

127

164 65.

165 1. The total of each horizontal line doubles from the outside to the centre.

166 40.

167 4. The total of each horizontal line doubles from the outside to the centre.

168 97.

169 12.

170 10.

171 15.

172 7.

173 41.

174 21.

175 15.

176 5.

177 50.

178 14.

179 47.

180 12.

181 8.

182

2	5	5	9
8	9	2	5
5	8	9	2
9	2	8	8

183 9.

184

7	3	3	7
6	4	6	4
3	6	3	7
4	7	6	4

185 22.

186

1	6	1	2	4
6	6	4	6	1
2	4	2	1	6
4	2	6	6	2
6	1	6	4	6

187 21.

188

9	8	4	3
3	5	8	5
4	4	3	9
3	5	8	4
9	8	9	5

189 30.

190

1	2	2	5	5	2
7	5	7	3	1	3
3	9	9	1	9	7
9	3	7	1	3	5
1	5	2	3	7	1
7	2	9	5	2	9

191 60.

192

2	9	5	5	1	6
4	8	1	9	5	2
7	3	6	2	7	8
6	3	7	1	7	3
1	8	2	8	3	4
9	5	4	4	6	9

193 3. The series reads 1, 2, 3, 1, 2, 3, etc.

194 4.

195 28. The numbers increase by 4 each time.

196 3.

197 16. The numbers increase by 3 each time.

198 5.

199 256. The numbers halve from the left each time.

200 8.

201 19. The series of numbers decreases from the left by 7, then 6, then 5, then 4, etc.

202 2.

203 5. Each number has its square root placed next to it.

204 5.

205 1 2 3 4 5 6. The numbers increase by 1 each time.

206 5 of 2V, 5V and 10V coins.

207 2 4 6 8 10 12. The numbers increase by 2 each time.

208 22 of 2V, 5V and 10V coins.

209 1 3 5 7 9 11. The numbers increase by 2 each time.

210 17 of 1V, 2V, 5V and 10V coins.

211 1 3 6 10 15 21. The numbers increase by 2, 3, 4, etc.

212 31 of 1V, 2V, 5V and 10V coins.

213 12 24 36 48 60 72. The numbers increase by 12 each time.

214 27 of 2V, 5V, 10V, 20V and 50V coins.

215 2 3 5 7 11 13. These are all prime numbers.

216 37 of 1V, 2V, 10V, 20V and 50V coins.

217 5.

218 2.

219 4.

★ YOUR PUZZLE NOTES ★

★ INTRODUCTION TO ★ WORD PUZZLES

I suppose you're not going to read this, are you? I mean, I don't blame you or anything, I'd probably do the same in your place. If you like messing about with words then by now you'll have plunged into the book unscrambling anagrams, crossing crosswords, sorting syllables and generally having fun. The puzzles are divided into six levels of difficulty from easy, Level A, to almost impossible, Level F. Work your way through each level. Even if the higher levels seem really difficult now, once you've done a few they'll seem less daunting.

Of course if you don't like words and a well-meaning relative bought this for you because they thought it was educational, then I'm sorry. It's not supposed to be educational. I hope it's engrossing, enchanting, delightful, tantalizing, tormenting and mind-bending. Have a quick look at the puzzles anyway. You never know, you might find out that you do like words after all.

If you like puzzles then you will probably like Mensa. It is the only society I know of which lets you in just because you are good at puzzling. We have over 100,000 members throughout the world. The great thing about Mensa is that you get to meet so many people with different interests.

We have what we call Special Interest Groups, which cover just about any subject you can imagine from Animal Rights to Science Fiction, or Artificial Intelligence to Star Trek. You need never be bored. So why not join? Full details are on page 7 of this book.

Many thanks to my friend Sarah Picken for her help in compiling this section of the book.

R. P. Allen

Robert Allen
Editorial Director
British Mensa

THUMB SUCKERS

★ LEVEL A ★

PUZZLE 1

Below you'll find a pyramid. Using the clues, fill in the correct words. To help you, to make the new word a letter is added to the end of the previous word each time.

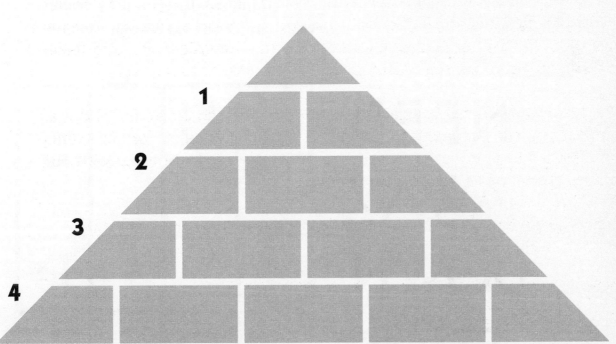

1. A term of endearment for your father.

2. You can cook dinner in this.

3. Found in a window.

4. A group of entertainers appearing as contestants in a TV quiz show.

ANSWER NO.54

PUZZLE 2

The sentence below is a well known quotation.
We have used a simple trick to obscure the meaning. Can you unscramble it?

WTOB ABEL FORC GNOTH ATOS OBER, ATHATI HIST ATHEM BQUESTIONA.

 ANSWER NO.63

PUZZLE 3

If you fill the four words into the grid in the correct order,
something found on the beach will be revealed in the shaded column. What is it?

NEED
AWAY
DOWN
SHOP

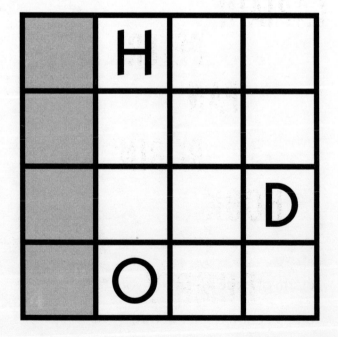

 ANSWER NO.81

PUZZLE 4

When animals are grouped together we have some very interesting names to describe the groups, for example a murder of crows. Here are some easy ones to get you started.

A – – – – of cows.

A – – – – – – of hens.

A – – – – – – of geese.

A – – – – – of lions.

A – – – – – – of fish.

 ANSWER NO.116

PUZZLE 5

Below you will find a number of characters from books and rhymes whose names have been mixed up. Can you put them together again and find the odd one out?

CAPTAIN

PETER

CHRISTOPHER

PAN

MOTHER

BETTY

ROBIN

HUMPTY

GOOSE

HOOK

BOTTER

DUMPTY

LUCY

 ANSWER NO.18

PUZZLE 6

The faces below have been made up out of letters.
If you unravel them you will find the names of the people.

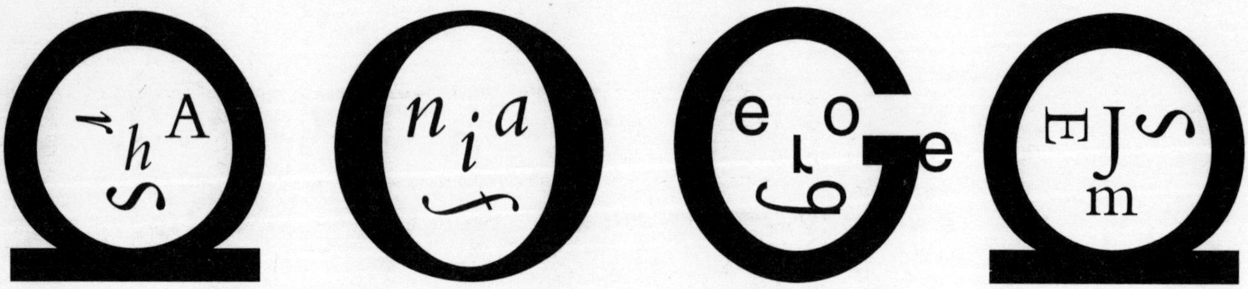
r h A s
n i a i f
e o r g e
E J s m

ANSWER NO.99

PUZZLE 7

What kind of a father goes round dressed all in red, and never cuts his beard, and works only one day a year? Unjumble the letters and you will find out

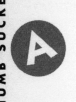

FATHER HSARSMITC

ANSWER NO.36

PUZZLE 8

One of these tins of paint does not go with the others, which is it?

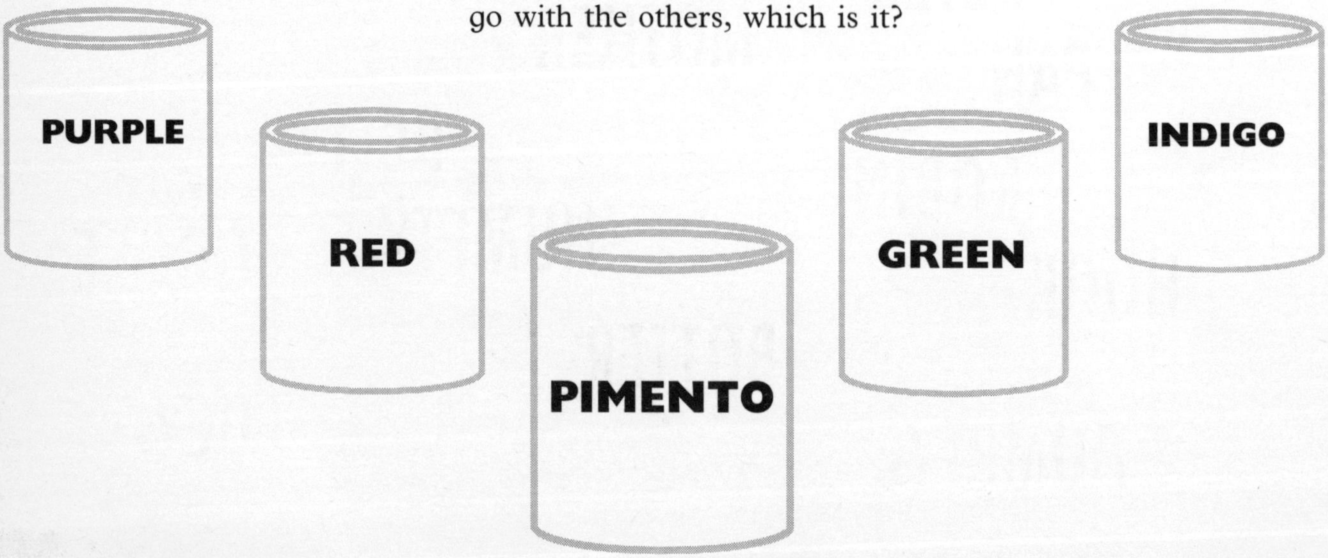
PURPLE
RED
PIMENTO
GREEN
INDIGO

ANSWER NO.125

PUZZLE 9

The clues below will help you to find words to fill the spaces.
To help you even more we can tell you that the first syllable of each word
could be found in a paint box.

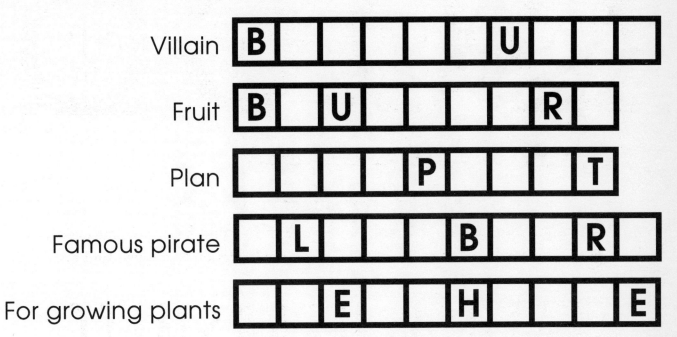

Villain   B _ _ _ U _ _

Fruit   B U _ _ _ R _

Plan   _ _ _ P _ _ T

Famous pirate _ L _ _ B _ R _

For growing plants _ _ E _ _ H _ _ E

 ANSWER NO.142

LEVEL A

PUZZLE 10

Below you'll find anagrams of four common pets. Which ones?

1. **tca**

2. **dgo**

3. **hifs**

4. **sahmter**

 ANSWER NO.167

PUZZLE 11

Who ate the grapes? Look at the word and see if you
can find a four-letter word describing the culprits.

ANSWER NO.27

PUZZLE 12

The bear had a sore head. He was not in a good mood.
In fact he was in a really awful mood. Take the jumbled letters below and
add them to the word bear to make one word which will show you just
how bad he was feeling.

E B N

L A U

- - - BEAR - - - - - -

ANSWER NO.45

PUZZLE 13

Fill in the words in the correct order and in the shaded column
you will be able to see something that comes out at night.

FORK
KNEE
POLE
OMEN

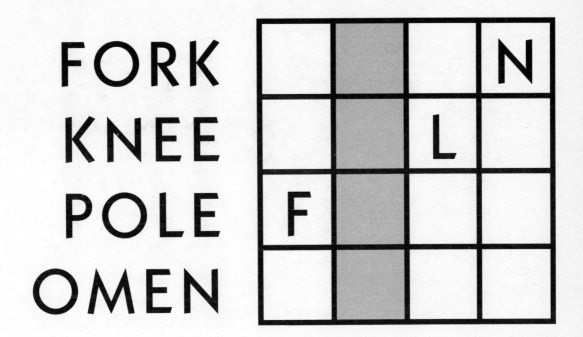

? ANSWER NO.80 ?

PUZZLE 14

If you solve these anagrams you will reveal four numbers.
What is the total of all the numbers added together?

1. ofur

2. vesen

3. noe

4. ixs

? ANSWER NO.98 ?

PUZZLE 15

Look at the words on the chalk board, which is the odd one out?

 ANSWER NO.9

PUZZLE 16

When rearranged, the anagrams below will turn into four types of weather.
Can you work out what they are?

1. **arin**

2. **usn**

3. **nsow**

4. **ahil**

 ANSWER NO.124

PUZZLE 17

Mrs Jones was very proud of her garden. She had the best asters in the county.
That is until next door's dog decided to bury his bone under them.
Add the three jumbled up letters to the front of the word aster
and make a new word telling you what happened.

_ _ _ ASTER

? ANSWER NO.141 ?

PUZZLE 18

The faces below have been made up out of letters.
If you unravel them you will find the names of the people.

? ANSWER NO.168 ?

LEVEL A

PUZZLE 19

The birds were just enjoying a few well-earned crumbs in the garden when along came that mean and murderous cat from the house round the corner. What did the birds do? Add the jumbled letters to the word cat and you will get the answer.

R   S

E   T

– C A T – – –

◆?◆ ANSWER NO.64 ◆?◆

PUZZLE 20

If you fill in these four words correctly you will find a type of flower in the shaded column.

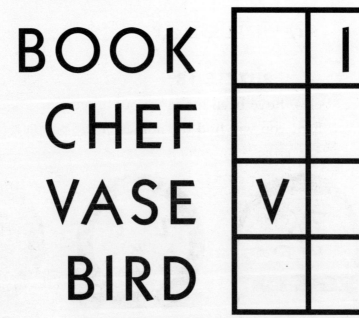

BOOK
CHEF
VASE
BIRD

◆?◆ ANSWER NO.151 ◆?◆

PUZZLE 21

At the zoo the monkeys were throwing oranges at each other.
If you look closely at the word orange you will see a three-letter word
which tells you what the keeper did.

<ANSWER NO.53>

PUZZLE 22

The planets in the night sky have an intruder
among them. Which is it?

EARTH

MARS

VERMICELLI

SATURN

MERCURY

<ANSWER NO.62>

143

THUMB SUCKERS

PUZZLE 23

Can you find the word ELEMENT? It appears only once
in a horizontal, vertical or diagonal line.

E	L	M	E	N	T	E	L	E	M
L	E	E	L	E	N	M	E	N	T
M	E	N	T	E	L	M	E	N	T
E	L	E	M	E	N	E	L	M	E
E	M	E	N	T	E	L	E	M	E
L	M	E	L	E	M	E	M	T	N
E	E	L	M	E	N	T	E	L	E
M	N	T	E	L	E	M	N	E	T
E	T	E	M	E	N	E	T	L	E
N	E	L	E	M	E	N	E	N	T

PUZZLE 24

It's bedtime but are you sleepy? No! Now what should we try?
Unravel the letters below and you will come up with a suggestion.

BEDTIME ROTSY

144

PUZZLE 25

Can you solve these anagrams to reveal four well-known parts of the body?

1. **ram**

2. **ahed**

3. **elg**

4. **ofot**

 ANSWER NO.17

PUZZLE 26

Have you had enough of school? Well, just unravel the jumbled letters and add them to the word play. Then relax.

PLAY EMIT

 ANSWER NO.100

PUZZLE 27

This is one strange dog! If you take the two groups of mixed-up letters and add one to the front and one to the end you will come up with the seven-letter names of two very different creatures.

L U L B H I S F

DOG

 ANSWER NO.35

145

Place the words into the grid in such a way that something hot can be seen in the shaded column.

ACHE

WOLF

HAIR

TAXI

ANSWER NO.126

PUZZLE 29

Look carefully at the caterpillar. See if you can find a three-letter word which tells you what happened to the apple. Caterpillars should only eat leaves, so he felt sick. See if you can also find a four-letter word which tells what he took to feel better.

CATERPILLAR

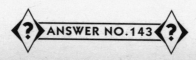
ANSWER NO.143

PUZZLE 30

Teddy isn't a boy and he isn't a dog, he isn't a tomato and he isn't a frog.
If you unravel the letters with care you will discover that he is a...

TEDDY AREB

ANSWER NO.166

PUZZLE 31

Take a look at the names on the children's school bags. Which is the odd one out?

ANSWER NO.26

PUZZLE 32

It was the highlight of the display. A giant firework! But what sort was it going to be?
Just unscramble the letters below to find the answer.

CATHERINE LEWEH

◈? ANSWER NO.44 ?◈

PUZZLE 33

Milo got into old Mr Jimson's orchard and guzzled his peaches happily all afternoon.
But that night the fruit had its revenge! Take a look at the word peaches and try to
find a five-letter word which describes just how Milo's tummy felt.

PEACHES

◈? ANSWER NO.79 ?◈

PUZZLE 34

Now we're really going to rock you! But how? With a track from the latest album by Total
Cosmic Disaster? Aren't you just a little young for that kind of music? Why not just
rearrange the jumbled letters below and come up with a swinging solution.

ROCKING SRHOE

◈? ANSWER NO.97 ?◈

THUMB SUCKERS

PENCIL CHEWERS

★ LEVEL B ★

PUZZLE 35

Look at the farm gate. It may look like alphabet soup to you but, if you start with the first H and then take every fifth letter, you will be able to find an animal who lives on the farm. Try again starting with the G, then the M and so on.

There are five hidden animals.

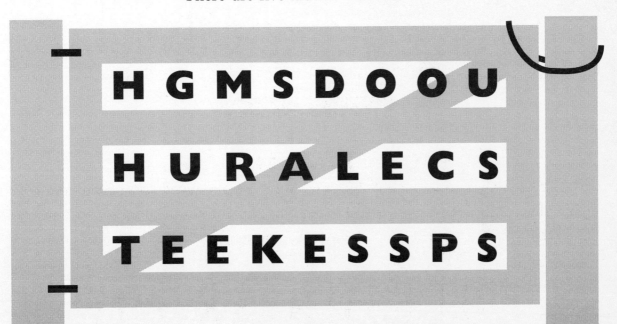

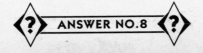
ANSWER NO.8

PUZZLE 36

Walter Foole has taken a job at the local library. Oh well, once a Foole always a Foole and he has already accidentally removed the name labels from several shelves. Try to sort them all out before the librarian finds out and marks Walter's card.

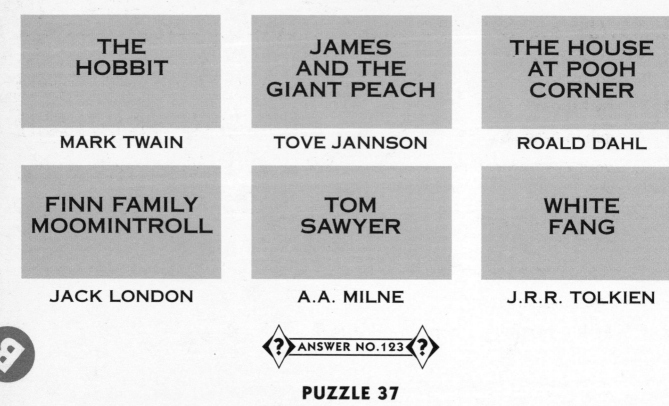

THE HOBBIT	JAMES AND THE GIANT PEACH	THE HOUSE AT POOH CORNER
MARK TWAIN	TOVE JANNSON	ROALD DAHL
FINN FAMILY MOOMINTROLL	TOM SAWYER	WHITE FANG
JACK LONDON	A.A. MILNE	J.R.R. TOLKIEN

◆?◆ ANSWER NO.123 ◆?◆

PUZZLE 37

Replace each question mark with a letter to form a word. Reading down you should discover the names of five things to be found in a kitchen. What are they?

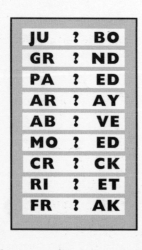

```
JU ? BO
GR ? ND
PA ? ED
AR ? AY
AB ? VE
MO ? ED
CR ? CK
RI ? ET
FR ? AK
```

```
BL ? OD
MO ? IE
FR ? SH
MA ? IA
```

```
HI ? ER
AM ? ND
OU ? ER
EX ? RA
SA ? TY
ST ? RN
```

```
WA ? ER
DI ? TY
RA ? NY
WE ? GE
AN ? ER
KN ? AD
```

```
HU ? KY
CR ? NE
AC ? TE
IN ? UR
TH ? ME
VE ? GE
```

◆?◆ ANSWER NO.140 ◆?◆

PENCIL CHEWERS

150

PUZZLE 38

All the well-known sayings have a word missing.
Complete them by taking words from the group on the right.

1. Too many chiefs and not enough ?

2. Many hands make ? work

3. An ? a day keeps the doctor away

4. A new broom ? clean

5. A stitch in time saves ?

6. Cut your coat according to your ?

7. When the ? away the mice will play

8. Can't see the wood for the ?

9. All's well that ends?

10. It's an ill ? that blows nobody any good

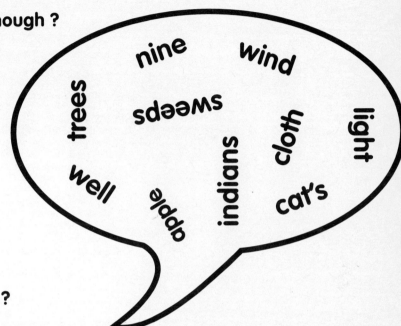

?◆ ANSWER NO.169 ◆?

LEVEL B

PUZZLE 39

The letters on the computer screen make a series.
Work out the logic and replace the question mark.

MTW
TFS?

?◆ ANSWER NO.65 ◆?

151

PUZZLE 40

The answers to the six clues below are all anagrams of each other. What are they?

Small piece of wire driven through
sheets of paper to hold them together.... ☐

A crayon for drawing .... ☐

The lightest hue .... ☐

You eat off them .... ☐

Folds often found in a girl's skirt .... ☐

The leaves of a flower .... ☐

 ANSWER NO.152

PUZZLE 41

Each of the following sets of clues should give you a pair of homophones
(words that sound the same but have different meanings).

B

NAKED		CARNIVORE
RODENT		BODY COVERING
DEER		BLOOD PUMP
BAMBI		BELOVED
PLANT		RECOGNISE WRITING
SUGAR PLANT		DEFEAT

 ANSWER NO.52

PUZZLE 42

The diagram shows a plan of the secret headquarters of the dreaded Crime Syndicate International. By following the instructions clearly you can reach the Boss's office and apprehend him. Exciting, isn't it?

Start at the square two places south of the one in the middle of the top line. Go 1 square east and 2 south. Now go 2 squares west and 4 north. The room you want is now 1 square SE.

Which is the final square?

A	B	C
D	E	F
G	H	I
J	K	L
M	N	O
P	Q	R

N
W↑E
S

 ANSWER NO.61

PUZZLE 43

The following sentence has two gaps which can be filled with words using the same seven letters.

The _ _ _ _ _ _ _ felt lonely on the frontier and longed for _ _ _ _ _ _ _ from home.

 ANSWER NO.83

PUZZLE 44

Replace each question mark with a letter to form a word. Reading down you should discover the names of five jobs. What are they?

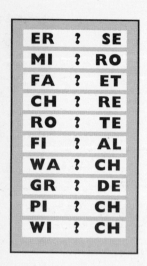

ER	?	SE
MI	?	RO
FA	?	ET
CH	?	RE
RO	?	TE
FI	?	AL
WA	?	CH
GR	?	DE
PI	?	CH
WI	?	CH

VI	?	AL
GR	?	ET
DR	?	WN
UL	?	ER
ET	?	IC
GL	?	AM
HO	?	SE

JU	?	GE
WH	?	RL
PA	?	TE
NI	?	HE
MA	?	OR
BR	?	WN
DE	?	AY
JO	?	ER
EV	?	NT
RO	?	AL

AM	?	LE
FR	?	SK
HO	?	LY
SH	?	RN
WI	?	TY

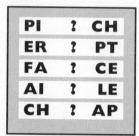

PI	?	CH
ER	?	PT
FA	?	CE
AI	?	LE
CH	?	AP

◆?▷ ANSWER NO.114 ◁?◆

PUZZLE 45

Add a letter anywhere along the length of each word to make another word which fits the clue. Taking the added letters in order, the name of a girl will be revealed. Which one?

- ☐ 1. SELL – an odour
- ☐ 2. MAD – a female servant
- ☐ 3. HEAP – not expensive
- ☐ 4. TANK – to show your gratitude
- ☐ 5. PACE – opposite of war
- ☐ 6. FOG – to beat severely
- ☐ 7. WED – to fuse bits of metal together by heating
- ☐ 8. BARD – hair found on the face

◆?▷ ANSWER NO.16 ◁?◆

PENCIL CHEWERS

B

PUZZLE 46

The creepie crawlies pictured have their names listed in code.
Just to make the game more interesting we have mixed them all up.
Leaving out "J", create a 5 x 5 grid with the letters A–E being A1 to A5,
F–K B1 to B5, etc. Use these codes to solve the puzzle.

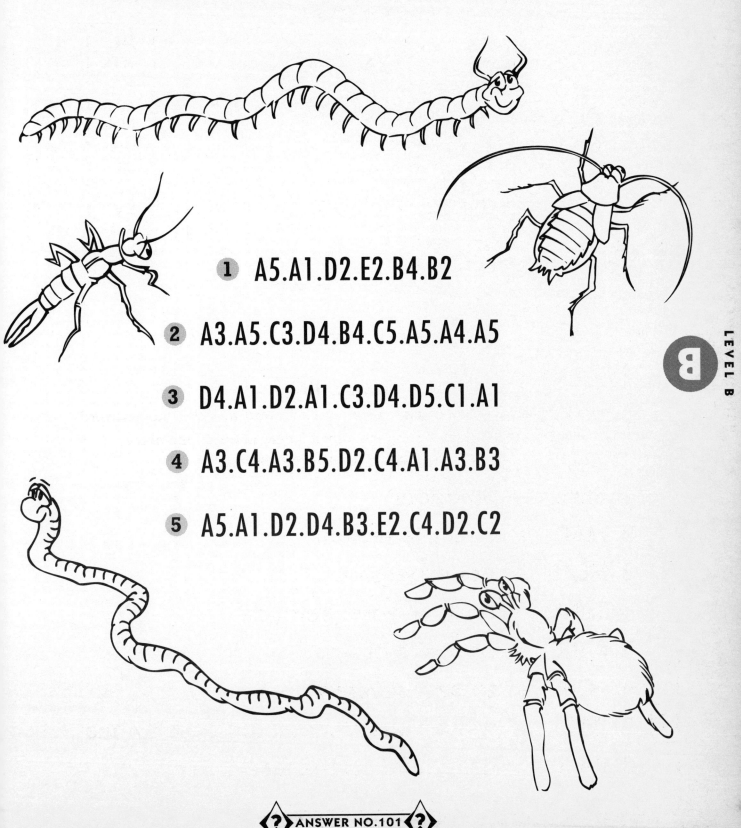

1 A5.A1.D2.E2.B4.B2

2 A3.A5.C3.D4.B4.C5.A5.A4.A5

3 D4.A1.D2.A1.C3.D4.D5.C1.A1

4 A3.C4.A3.B5.D2.C4.A1.A3.B3

5 A5.A1.D2.D4.B3.E2.C4.D2.C2

ANSWER NO.101

LEVEL B

B

Can you work out the five words below?

1. 3D 3B 1C 2D 3C

2. 3E 3D 2A 3A 1D

3. 1B 3B 2C 1E 1D

4. 1A 3C 2A 1B 3D

5. 2B 2C 1B 2D 3B

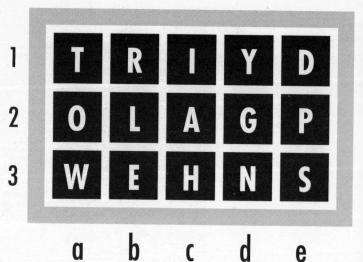

ANSWER NO.34

PUZZLE 48

We have taken some common expressions and mixed them up.
Try to sort them into their proper sequence.

PENCIL CHEWERS

TO SWIM CATS AND DOGS

TO FLY LIKE A ROSE

TO RAIN LIKE THE WIND

TO RUN LIKE A FISH

TO SMELL LIKE A BIRD

ANSWER NO.127

PUZZLE 49

The following are nicknames which have been mixed up.
Some of them belong to things and some to people. When you have
sorted them out you should find one pair which doesn't fit.

BIG | BRIAN
OLD | BEARD
UNION | NORMAN
BLUE | GLORY
GREEN | BEN
STORMIN' | JACK

 ANSWER NO.144

PUZZLE 50

Find the letter to place at the centre of the wheel which will turn
all the spokes into five-letter words. Each word starts with the same letter.

 ANSWER NO.165

PUZZLE 51

In a twisted, mind-bending sort of way the following words form a series.
Which is the odd one out?

Adverb

Card

Engulf

Become

Grouch

ANSWER NO.25

PUZZLE 52

In Madame Twoswords' famous waxworks Walter Foole,
the newest assistant, has mixed up the labels on the dummies.
Can you sort them out and help this dummy keep his job?

OLIVER	WASHINGTON
MAHATMA	ROBERTS
MICHELLE	CROMWELL
GEORGE	GANDHI
ROBIN	PFEIFFER
JULIA	CODY
WILLIAM	HOOD

ANSWER NO.43

PUZZLE 53

Add one letter to each line which will end the left word and start the right word, changing both into new English words. Reading down, a popular star from the world of sport will be revealed. Which one?

	?	
SAG	?	WASH
THROW	?	ARROW
FIRE	?	ARK
PRIME	?	ANGER
HER	?	LOPE
DRAM	?	VERSION
BE	?	RATE
ARE	?	BATE
FORGE	?	CUBA
PEN	?	LEDGE
YET	?	RATE

ANSWER NO.78

LEVEL B

PUZZLE 54

The answers to the five clues below are all anagrams of one another.
What are the words?

Something left over................................ ☐

Fruits that grow on trees...................... ☐

He clears the field of a crop.................. ☐

She cuts off the outer surface.............. ☐

Ancient battle weapon .... ☐

ANSWER NO.96

PUZZLE 55

It is now Walter's second day working at the world renowned waxworks of Madame Twoswords and he's gone and mixed up the first names and surnames of the models. Having sorted the labels into equal piles, can you help put them in the right order before Madame has poor Walter coated in wax and put on display.

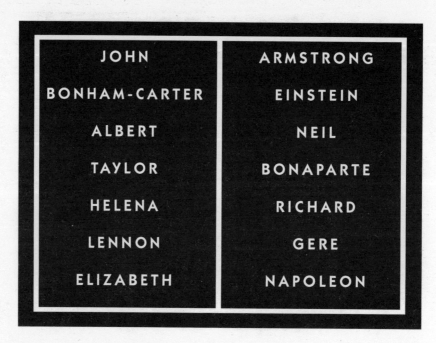

JOHN	ARMSTRONG
BONHAM-CARTER	EINSTEIN
ALBERT	NEIL
TAYLOR	BONAPARTE
HELENA	RICHARD
LENNON	GERE
ELIZABETH	NAPOLEON

ANSWER NO.7

PUZZLE 56

The answers to these ten clues all rhyme. What are they?

1. Reptile or unpleasant person. [ ]
2. A dull persistent pain. [ ]
3. One way to cook potatoes. [ ]
4. An implement used in the garden. [ ]
5. To rouse from sleep [ ]
6. To abandon someone. [ ]
7. A large body of water. [ ]
8. To fracture an arm. [ ]
9. Marker in the ground. [ ]
10. To falsify. [ ]

ANSWER NO.122

PUZZLE 57

The answers to the five clues below all rhyme.

What are they?

1. Unswerving in allegiance.
2. To ruin.
3. Their blood might be blue.
4. Hard work.
5. Grotesque spout on roof.

 ANSWER NO.139

PUZZLE 58

You are hunting the autograph of Mucho Macho the film star.

You know the right street but not the number.

Here are some clues to help you find the house.

1. Mucho is much too macho to have flowers in his garden.

2. The number of the house cannot be divided by 7.

3. The house is not called Sunshine Cottage.

4. If the house number is divided by two the result is between 15 and 17.

5. Mucho made a film called 'Moon Mission'. It bombed.

6. Mucho is a known cat lover.

 ANSWER NO.170

LEVEL B

NAIL NIBBLERS

★ LEVEL C ★

PUZZLE 59

The following strings of letters are all anagrams of well known cities. But each one contains an extra letter. Throw all the extra letters in the bin and you will have the name of one of the States of America.

dilnono

rapids

amore

shallad

oookyt

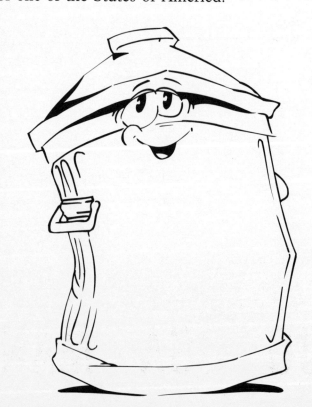

ANSWER NO.66

162

PUZZLE 60

Remove ten letters to leave a dead language.

C A L S B A R E T T I P N O R

ANSWER NO.153

PUZZLE 61

The letters below spell out six three-letter words. The letters of each word are in different type styles but always in the same order. The order is this

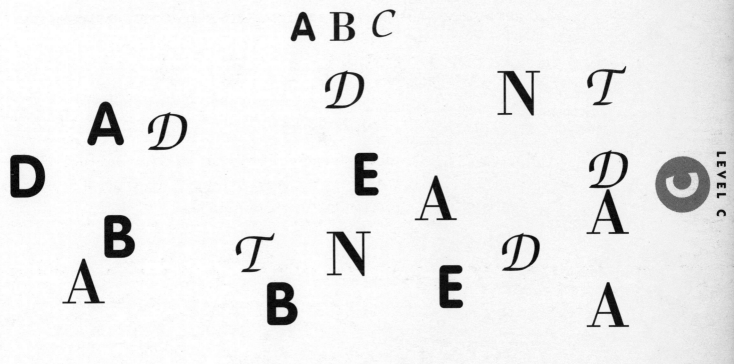

ANSWER NO.51

LEVEL C

PUZZLE 62

The following groups of letters are all names of countries from which two-letter 'heads' and 'tails' have been removed. How many can you recognise?

RTUG   NGA   MAN   RMA   EE

ANSWER NO.60

PUZZLE 63

Solve the clues and write the answers in the appropriate boxes.
The right-hand answer will always be the same as the left-hand answer, except that one letter will be missing. Write the missing letter in the box on the far right, and reading down you will discover the name of a sauce.

1. DIsplay
2. Pig
3. Shop available for business
4. What you write with
5. Not the back
6. Place for baptism
7. Mad
8. Silly
9. Awareness of danger
10. A long way
11. A fish
12. Hat
13. Tidy
14. Device for catching fish
15. Wet
16. Unit of electrical current
17. Falling water
18. Was in the race
19. Someone who annoys
20. Domestic animal
21. Blow with axe
22. Policeman

1		2		
3		4		
5		6		
7		8		
9		10		
11		12		
13		14		
15		16		
17		18		
19		20		
21		22		

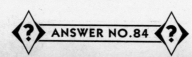 ANSWER NO.84

PUZZLE 64

Find a four-letter word which can be added to the end of the words of the left-hand column and the beginning of the words in the right-hand column to give 10 new words.

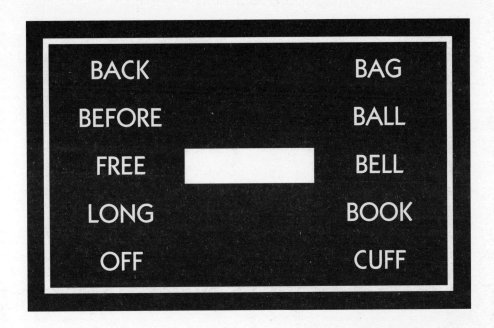

BACK	BAG
BEFORE	BALL
FREE	BELL
LONG	BOOK
OFF	CUFF

? ANSWER NO.113 ?

PUZZLE 65

Re-arrange the letters in the grid to find the name of a computer game hero.

S	C	E	E
T	N	H	O
D	I	H	G
O	H	E	G

? ANSWER NO.15 ?

PUZZLE 66

Identify the animals and fish concealed among the letters.
The words may run in any direction and may overlap.

T	A	B	E	A	R	G	S	G	A
P	C	O	D	F	O	T	S	H	B
A	G	O	T	R	Q	U	N	V	D
R	T	H	F	L	M	N	A	W	R
R	C	I	D	E	S	A	K	K	A
O	R	S	G	T	U	N	E	L	P
T	A	V	T	E	C	B	O	P	O
U	G	Z	Q	S	R	L	J	R	E
H	I	Y	E	K	N	O	M	E	L
C	E	L	E	P	H	A	N	T	D

ANSWER NO. 102

PUZZLE 67

Find a word or name that goes with the one we have given and then read down the first letter of each answer. You should find a nameless word!

	pie
	conquest
	singer
	watchman
	fever
	Twain
	poppy
	duckling
	spray

 **ANSWER NO.33**

PUZZLE 68

The letters written on the petals contain anagrams of five common wild flowers. Can you name them?

RIMSO REP

PTUTB UCRE

SAYID

HRTA EEH

LULBE EBL

ANSWER NO.128

PUZZLE 69

Below you'll find a list of words containing 'E' as their only vowel.
Can you locate them in the big 'E' shape? Which is the word that appears twice?

BEETLE	EFFECT	HERE	MESSENGER	PEPPER	TEPEE
CEMETERY	ENTENTE	JESTER	MERGE	REFEREE	VESSEL
CLEVER	FERMENT	KESTREL	METHYLENE	REFERENCE	WHEREVER
CRESCENT	GREENERY	LETTER	NEEDLE	SEETHE	YEN
DETERGENT	HELMET	MEDLEY	NETTLES	THEME	

```
M Y R E F E R E N C E N R Y R R K E
E E N V E S E R E V E R E H W W E S
S N E C E F F E C T Y M T E S S S E
Y T E E G E R F L S E E T E N N R S
R S D N R K E R E H S F E D B B N P
E E L S E R J E T E F E L T H H Y E
N J E S M R E
E H T E E S Y
E E N T J E T B Y F L E C H T E K R
R T P N Y E E R F E S E L T T E N E
G R E E T P M T E P L G E N E R E P
F R E G N E S S E M R D V E V C F P
E V T R E T L E T E M L E E H R F E
E E N E C P R R E M S E R L M Y R P
L Y K T S P E
C R R E E K H
V E E D R E C E B E V G Y F E E R I
E T T F C S E E N E L Y H T E M H E
T E S S E T F L S M E T S E C S E M
E M E E F R F S T E S T E M L E H E
N E J R B E E T R E F E L X J V E H
T C E C R L M E T N E T N E E N E T
```

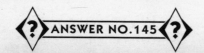
ANSWER NO.145

PUZZLE 70

Solve the clues and you will find that the first letter of the answers make a word when read down. Clue: May be shocking.

Clue	Answer
Natural force	
Greater in length	
Live coal	
British sport	
Medicine in pill form	
Herb with girl's name	
Herb found in pizza	
Walk slowly	
Never-ending	

 ANSWER NO.164

PUZZLE 71

When you solve these clues and fill the answers into the grid you will find that it reads the same down and across.

1. **Not slow.**

2. **A particular piece of ground.**

3. **In a tennis match there are a maximum of five.**

4. **A piece of work to be done.**

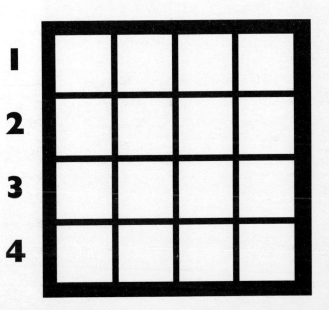

 ANSWER NO.24

The new postman has been given an important parcel to deliver to the house of Pearl Precious, the movie star. He doesn't know the exact number of the house but the guys at the sorting office have given him a few clues. See if you can help him to find the right house

NAIL NIBBLERS

1. Pearl Precious has no pets.

2. The number of her house cannot be divided by 3.

3. Pearl does not have milk delivered.

4. Pearl hates flowers.

5. The number of the house is not a prime number.

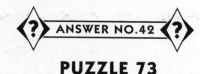

ANSWER NO.42

PUZZLE 73

Put a word in the middle space which makes, when added to the end of the words on the left and the beginning of the words on the right, eight new eight-letter words.

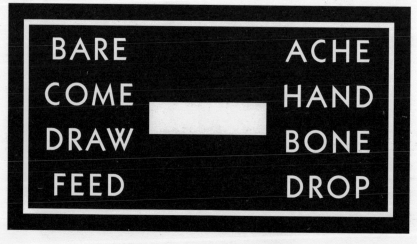

BARE   ACHE
COME   HAND
DRAW   BONE
FEED   DROP

ANSWER NO.77

Take a letter from each cloud in turn and make four words connected with bad weather.

◇ ? ANSWER NO.95 ? ◇

PUZZLE 75

When you have solved all the clues, read the first letter of the answers and you will find a hidden word. The clue is a mystery.

Clue	
Violet	
Quantity	
Agreement	
Athletic competition	
Sub-continent	
Adhesive	
Wet weather gear	
Pachyderm	

ANSWER NO.6

PUZZLE 76

The diagram shows the front of a very clever type of safe.
Turn each wheel in the order given and you will be able to open the door.
What is the proper order?

The final square is to the south of the square two places east of the square which is one place due south of the square at the extreme north west.

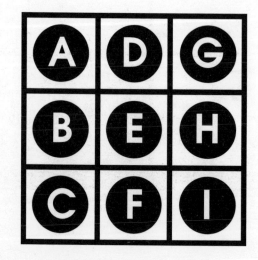

ANSWER NO.121

PUZZLE 77

Eight kids are hiding in the grid below hoping to avoid school.
Their names are: PETE, SUSIE, DICK, MICHELLE, JOSH,
HOLLY, LARRY, and JULIA. Can you find them?
The names may be spelt in any direction, not necessarily in a straight line..

J	H	A	C	D	J	U	L	V	Q
O	S	R	T	S	U	L	N	I	P
A	P	V	D	N	E	S	I	E	A
N	E	W	K	I	P	Q	U	R	H
C	T	E	L	J	C	S	O	G	T
Y	Q	T	E	I	U	K	Z	X	C
R	E	L	L	E	H	C	I	M	R
R	V	A	K	L	T	E	B	O	J
A	T	U	H	O	L	L	Y	Y	S
L	K	L	H	O	P	R	U	T	G

LEVEL C

ANSWER NO.138

173

PUZZLE 78

The following sentences have been written in a special way to hide their meaning.
If you look at them carefully you may get the message.

RGELA HANTSELEP DOMSEL KLWA CKLYQUI

TERSHAMS ERNEV KETA NCHLU THWI DILESCROCO

ENEV LLSMA FFESGIRA EPSLE DINGSTAN

IFULBEAUT RFLIESBUTTE TERFLIT ONGAM WERSFLO

ANTGI DASPAN ELLDW ONGAM BOOBAM VESGRO

ANSWER NO.171

PUZZLE 79

The following are books in which the words have been jumbled.
Can you sort them out?

THE OF
MOHICANS
LAST
THE

PRAIRIE
THE HOUSE
LITTLE
THE ON

CENTRE
THE TO
EARTH OF
JOURNEY
TO

THOUSAND
SEA UNDER
LEAGUES
TWENTY
THE

SERVICE
HER
SECRET
MAJESTY'S
ON

ANSWER NO.67

PUZZLE 80

When you have solved the clues you will find that the first letter of the answers will give a hidden word reading down.

Instrument for giving commands		
Assault		
Fighting vehicle		
Strategy		
Not yet a captain		
Foe		

Clue: Part of a war

 ANSWER NO.154

PUZZLE 81

The jumbled words in the bubbles are all languages.
How many can you unscramble?

HCSENIE

CARBIA

NALIAIT

GHELSNI

PHSINAS

 ANSWER NO.50

The letters on the side of the glue pot make the word adhesives.
How many words of four letters or more can you make out of the nine letters given?

ANSWER NO.59

PUZZLE 83

The answer to each line becomes part of the clue to the next one.
What are the seven words?

The first word is good to spend;

Change the first letter for something to eat;

Add a letter in front for a sham;

Drop the last letter to have a long-distance chat;

Drop the first letter, change the third for where you live;

Change the third but don't fall in this;

Change the first letter to leave you with a burrowing animal.

ANSWER NO.85

NAIL NIBBLERS

PUZZLE 84

The words below have had letters replaced by playing card symbols. Each symbol always stands for the same letter. Can you work out what the words should be? We have given some clues to help.

BU♥♥♠♦ — yellow spread

♥O♥♥♠♦ — unsteady walk

BA♦♦♠♣ — contains water?

♣ONG♠♦ — increased length

♦UBB♣♠♠ — broken stones

♥O♥A♣S — sums

ANSWER NO.112

LEVEL C

PUZZLE 85

This fairy tale character became confused after failing to recognise her grandmother. Can you sort her out?

EIGHT TENDRIL IDOL ROD

ANSWER NO.14

PUZZLE 86

The sentences below conceal the names of countries.
All the letters are in the right order.

The names are well hidden, mark my words!
I can adamantly state you will not find them.
It will anger many of you to search in vain.
But do not let your ire land you in trouble.
Attack the problem with new zeal and
overcome it.

PUZZLE 87

Each of the groups of words below has an odd one out.
Can you find them all?

CHEESE MILK BUTTER EGGS	JANUARY SEPTEMBER AUGUST DECEMBER	SPIDER ANT CRICKET BUTTERFLY	ENGLAND SPAIN GREECE POLAND
CALIFORNIA UTAH TEXAS NOVA SCOTIA	JAGUAR LINCOLN HARLEY- DAVIDSON PORSCHE	GANGES THAMES MISSISSIPPI CAMBRIDGE	CUMULUS NIMBUS CYCLONE STRATUS

NAIL NIBBLERS

PUZZLE 88

Below are ten clues. To help you solve them,
we've supplied the vowels for each answer.

1. To turn about on a axis   `[ ] [O] [ ] [A] [ ] [E]`

2. Juicy   `[ ] [U] [ ] [U] [ ] [E] [ ]`

3. Helps after dinner   `[ ] [I] [ ] [ ] [A] [ ] [E] [ ]`

4. Unfriendly   `[ ] [O] [ ] [I] [ ] [E]`

5. Of the night   `[ ] [O] [ ] [U] [ ] [A] [ ]`

6. A border between two countries   `[ ] [ ] [O] [ ] [I] [E]`

7. To tear roughly   `[ ] [A] [ ] [E] [ ] [A] [ ] [E]`

8. To unroll a flag   `[U] [ ] [ ] [U] [ ] [ ]`

9. To have an unjust opinion of   `[ ] [I] [ ] [ ] [U] [ ] [E]`

10. Four times a year   `[ ] [U][A] [ ] [E] [ ] [ ] [ ]`

?◆ ANSWER NO.129 ◆?

PUZZLE 89

The answer to each line becomes part of the clue to the next one.
What are the seven words?

The first word has already been said;

Remove the third letter for a clenched hand;

Jumble the letters to put through a sieve;

Change the first to raise weights in sport and body building;

Jumble the letters to fly from here to there;

Remove the second to be in good shape;

Change the last for an edible fruit.

?◆ ANSWER NO.146 ◆?

LEVEL C

PUZZLE 90

Below you'll find a list of rock and pop stars. All of them, except one, can be found hidden in the word search. Which one is missing? The names you have to find may be written forwards, backwards, upwards, downwards or diagonally.

Alexander O'Neal	**Debbie Gibson**	**New Kids on the Block**
Amy Grant	**En Vogue**	**Prince**
Belinda Carlisle	**Heart**	**REM**
Billy Joel	**Jade**	**Richard Marx**
Bobby Brown	**Janet Jackson**	**Right Said Fred**
Bon Jovi	**Madonna**	**Take That**
Bruce Springsteen	**Mariah Carey**	**Whitney Houston**
Cathy Dennis	**Martika**	**Wilson Philips**
Cher	**Michael Jackson**	

```
D A M E G O N O S B I G E I B B E D O I
A Y I D U T T S P R I N G W H C A M S L
X O C G O H A N N O D A M R N A K O L L
M C H H D G K D A J B U N I Y T I D A J
I S A P E I E U P R I R R G E Z T E E D
N P E W O R T V E I G P E H R I R L N E
O I L S P Y H I E D F Y O T A R A L O L
T L J N I R A F A O A D M S C P M I R S
S L A O T N T I T Z G J V A H M X B E I
U I C B E E N V O G U E U I A E E K D L
O H K C O L B E H T N O S D I K W E N R
H P S D S O C E D A B E S F R A K E A A
Y N O A S O A R I Y F A N R A R C H X C
E O N J R R I Z E R H N O E M A A C E A
N S C E T V A Y A M E T D D V T J N L D
T L E R O N X R A M D R A H C I R I A N
I I Q J N E W K P H I L M C A K T B L I
H W N E E T S G N I R P S E C U R B A L
W O J B O B B Y B R O W N H A M E N P E
B E Q U I V A R K L P L E O J Y L L I B
```

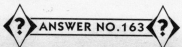

ANSWER NO. 163

PUZZLE 91

The words of these famous proverbs have been jumbled up.
Can you unravel them?

1 Lady never won fair faint heart.

2 The bush is worth in the two hand in a bird.

3 No spilt crying it's milk use over.

4 Glass shouldn't live in stones houses who throw people.

 ANSWER NO.23

PUZZLE 92

Try to find out the name of this fairy tale character.
Come to think of it, that was the point of the story!

SLIP MILK ENTRUST

 ANSWER NO.41

PUZZLE 93

These film titles are written without vowels.
Your task is to find the missing vowels and reveal the film.

1. TH WZRD F Z
2. CLS NCNTRS F TH THRD KND
3. PLLYNN
4. BCK T TH FTR
5. NTNL VLVT
6. BTMN RTRNS
7. BTY ND TH BST
8. HNY SHRNK TH KDS
9. TH SND F MSC
10. JRSSC PRK

 ANSWER NO.176

PUZZLE 94

By moving one square up, down, right or left – not diagonally – follow the trail of letters in the grid and you will find the title of a Steven Spielberg film. But beware, there are six dummy letters included.

 ANSWER NO.94

PUZZLE 95

This kid stayed out late and lost her footing. Can you unscramble her
and give the tale a happy ending?

ANSWER NO.5

PUZZLE 96

The words below spell out four well-known phrases. The first word of each line is
in the right place but the others have been mixed up so that, although the word is
in the right place within a line, it has been moved up or down and is now in the wrong line.
You have to sort them out. To help you there is a clue for each line.

Here	big	the	she	and	grand	bush
What	lion	eyes	you	lost	her	wardrobe
The	Bo	go	witch	have	mulberry	sheep
Little	we	Peep	round	the	the	mama

Clues: Line 1. Nursery Rhyme
Line 2. Little Red Riding Hood
Line 3. Narnia
Line 4. Careless Shepherdess

ANSWER NO.120

PUZZLE 97

Can you decipher these film titles?

1 Excellent and Adventure Ted's Bill.

2 Eighty in Around Days World the.

3 of Purple Cairo The Rose.

4 an Stepmother My Alien is.

5 Being Importance The Earnest of.

 ANSWER NO.137

PUZZLE 98

The following proverbs have been rewritten using a long word or words where a short one would have been better! See if you can work out what we mean.

1. It is a malicious shift of atmospheric pressure which fails to produce benefits for some members of the population.

2. A surfeit of hard labour unmixed with recreational activities has the unfortunate effect of making Jack a rather uninteresting youth.

3. An excessive number of culinary operatives tends to have an extremely adverse effect upon the quality of the pottage.

4. It is said to be impossible to fabricate a money-holding device of fine cloth from the aural appendage of a porcine quadruped.

5. When precipitation occurs it has a marked tendency to do so in excessive quantities.

 ANSWER NO.172

How well do you know stage musicals, old and new? Below you'll find some of them with their vowels missing. Can you work out what the musicals should be?

1. PHNTM F TH PR
2. CRSL
3. VT
4. STRLGHT XPRSS
5. TH SND F MSC
6. LS MSRBLS
7. CHSS
8. MSS SGN
9. RCKY HRRR SHW
10. CTS

 ANSWER NO.68

PUZZLE 100

This fairy tale character was a bit of a bird brain.
Maybe that's how she got so confused.

ANSWER NO.155

185

Can you find the ten movies hidden in the passage below?

I often visit my cousin on a Friday afternoon. On this particular occasion she was doodling on a piece of green card when I arrived. I couldn't be sure (she's not exactly famous for her artistic talents!) but her drawing seemed to be of a group of gorillas. In the mist outside her window I could just make out her dog frolicking in the flowerbeds.

As was her custom, my cousin made me a cup of tea. I don't know about you, but I can't drink tea until it's cooled off a bit. Some like it hot, but I'm certainly not one of them!

"Who's that girl?" I inquired, pointing at a photograph that was perched on top of her television.

"That's Hannah – and her sisters are in the other photo over there. Hannah's a mannequin – it's a wonderful life for her, you know. In the world of fashion modelling she's a real star.

Wars may happen, natural disasters change the face of the earth as we know it , but Hannah will always be a success. By contrast, her sisters do little – women, they believe, shouldn't leave the kitchen sink."

ANSWER NO.49

PUZZLE 102

The words below spell out four well-known phrases. The first word of each line is in the right place but the others have been mixed up so that, although the word is in the right place within a line, it has been moved up or down and is now in the wrong line. You have to sort them out. To help you there is a clue for each line.

The	does	and	Pooh	king
The	huff	at	future	puff
How	house	your	I'll	Corner
I'll	once	and	garden	grow

Clues: Line 1. King Arthur
Line 2. Christopher Robin
Line 3. Contrary Gardener
Line 4. Big Bad threat

 ANSWER NO.58

PUZZLE 103

The following are well-known books
disguised in newspaper headlines.

GIRL IN RABBIT
HOLE DRAMA
CLAIMS BIZARRE
ADVENTURE

MISSISSIPPI
BOY –
PRESUMED DEAD
– RETURNS WITH
TREASURE

TRANSYLVANIAN
COUNT WANTED
ON ASSAULT
CHARGES FLEES
TO ENGLAND

MARINER
CLAIMS STRANGE
ADVENTURE
AMONG TINY
PEOPLE

SMALL BOY
IN MOUSE
TRANSFORMATION.
SHOCKING
WITCHCRAFT
ALLEGATION

 ANSWER NO.86

PUZZLE 104

Here are some more proverbs disguised with pompous phrasing and long words. Simplify!

1. Everything which reflects sparkling brilliance is not necessarily composed of a precious, malleable, ductile metallic element.

2. A concretion of mineral matter incessantly turning upon its surface is extremely unlikely to acquire a collection of small primitive plants.

3. Herbage always appears to have a more intense shade of verdancy when it is seen upon the far side of a boundary marker.

4. In order to apprehend someone who misappropriates the property of others it is necessary to retain the services of a person engaged in the same profession.

5. It is a strange fact that vexatious circumstances always appear to arrive as triplets.

 ANSWER NO.111

PUZZLE 105

Can you work out what these proverbs are supposed to be?
One word of each proverb can be found in each column.

Too	stitch	rains	but	it	day
A	many	built	feather	a	broth
It	wasn't	cooks	in	flock	pours
Rome	of	a	time	saves	together
Birds	never	in	spoil	the	nine

 ANSWER NO.13

PUZZLE 106

Here are some book titles in which all the consonants have been removed. Can you work out the titles just from the vowels? It's rather difficult, so we've given a clue to each one.

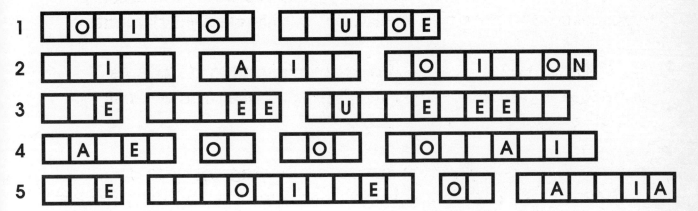

1. Desert Island.
2. Another island, same name!
3. All for one!
4. Hobbit friend
5. Aslan

 ANSWER NO.104

PUZZLE 107

What is the musical instrument hidden in the riddle?

My first is in PROMISE, but not in PRIZE

My second's in ACTOR, but not COMPROMISE

My third is in EXCELLENCE, but not in OVER

My fourth is in ORANGE, and also in CLOVER

My fifth is in SLOPE, but not in GREASE

My sixth is in SHELF, but not in PEACE

My seventh's in POLITE, and also in POINT

My eighth is in TONGUE, and also ANOINT

My ninth is in GRAPE, but not in GONG

And here is the end of my silly song!

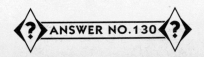 ANSWER NO.130

PUZZLE 108

The words on the scales of the monster are an anagram of a
dinosaur name though, needless to say, it is not the one pictured.
Can you work out which big beast is hidden in the puzzle?

ANSWER NO.31

HEAD BANGERS

★ LEVEL D ★

PUZZLE 109

If you add the same letter to the end of the left word and the start of the right one on each line, you will find the name of a famous film star reading down. Who is he?

STAR	?	WINE
CELL	?	MISSION
FAR	?	ASK
AMNESIA	?	REST
ANGLE	?	AFTER
MEN	?	NIT
CHILL	?	SLAM
TUB	?	HOE
SHIN	?	BONY

ANSWER NO.147

191

PUZZLE 110

My first is in TIGER, but not in CAT
My second's in UGLY, but not ACROBAT
My next is in UMBRELLA, and also in BELL
My fourth is in OWL, but not in JEWEL
My fifth and my fourth are two peas in a pod
My whole is a dwelling that some may find odd

◆?◆ ANSWER NO.162 ◆?◆

PUZZLE 111

The names of three creatures often found as pets have been mixed up.
All the letters are in the right order.

D G O
O
R A G
L
D B B
F
I I T S
H

◆?◆ ANSWER NO.22 ◆?◆

PUZZLE 112

The following figures, representing certain letters, make up a ten letter word:

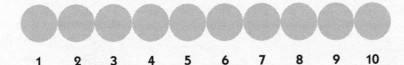

1   2   3   4   5   6   7   8   9   10

Your task is to work out the above word by making use of the clues below.

 *means* a list specifying a fixed order

 *means* part of the nose

 *means* a lion's home

 *means* combat on horseback

ANSWER NO.40

PUZZLE 113

LEVEL D

Below you'll find the names of five birds which all start from the central C.
The letters which make up the words are connected vertically, horizontally and diagonally.
Not every letter is used and some may be used more than once. What are the birds?

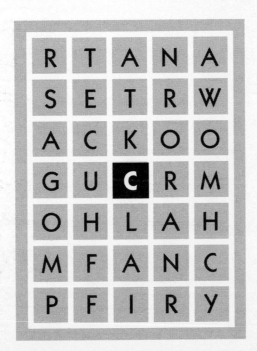

ANSWER NO.75

PUZZLE 114

The unpronounceable jumbles below are really States in America without their vowels.
How many of them can you unravel?

⟨?⟩ ANSWER NO.93 ⟨?⟩

PUZZLE 115

All the answers to the clues below are five-letter words.
When you have written them in the grid, you will be able to read the names
of two signs of the zodiac down the first and last columns. Which ones?

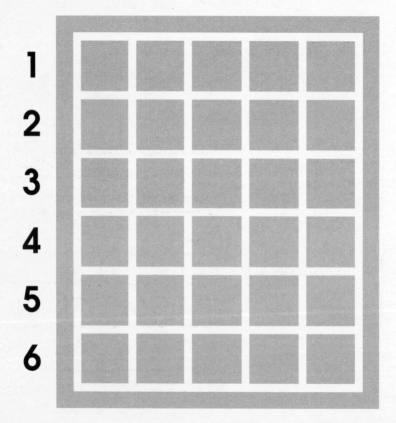

1. To move around quietly
2. Someone who says you were with them when the crime was committed.

3. You have these on fingers and toes.
4. Man who makes you laugh as his job.

5. Bird of prey.
6. A train runs on these.

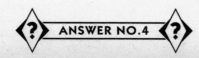⟨?⟩ ANSWER NO.4 ⟨?⟩

PUZZLE 116

All the words in the left-hand box have something in common. Which of the words in the right-hand box should join them?

DRAPERY	SPEND
COWARD	SAUCER
SPIGOT	CATAPULT
DOGGED	BICYCLE

◆ ANSWER NO. 119 ◆

PUZZLE 117

Below are ten clues. To help you we've supplied the consonants for each answer.

LEVEL D

1. Not straightforward
   `_ B L _ Q _ _`

2. The unlimited extent of space
   `_ N F _ N _ T Y`

3. Conceit
   `_ R R _ G _ N C _`

4. To recover after sickness
   `C _ N V _ L _ S C _`

5. A period of 1000 years
   `M _ L L _ N N _ _ M`

6. Having effects below the level of conscious awareness
   `S _ B L _ M _ N _ L`

7. Having human characteristics
   `H _ M _ N _ _ D`

8. Inventiveness
   `_ N G _ N _ _ T Y`

9. Basic
   `R _ D _ M _ N T _ R Y`

10. A bunch of flowers
    `B _ _ Q _ _ T`

◆ ANSWER NO. 136 ◆

195

As you can see, a shark has been at work. He's chewed up a lot of fish and left their spare syllables scattered on the sea bed. However, you may be able to save the situation by putting the syllables back together again to form the names of five kinds of fish.
Which is the one left over?

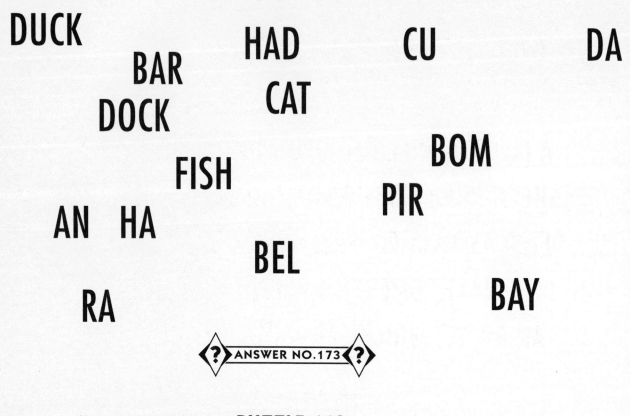

DUCK HAD CU DA

BAR

DOCK CAT

BOM

FISH PIR

AN HA

BEL

RA BAY

?ANSWER NO.173?

PUZZLE 119

Can you find a nine-letter word scrambled in the square?
Clue: A bit jumpy.

?ANSWER NO.69?

PUZZLE 120

Your first task is to solve the clues below. When you have your seven answers, you'll find these letters also contain the names of five breeds of dog. Which breeds?

CLUES

GREAT JOY AND HIGH SPIRITS   _ _ _ _ _ _ _

EVERYTHING   _ _ _

A PIECE OF INCLINED GROUND   _ _ _ _ _

SPAGHETTI IS AN EXAMPLE OF THIS   _ _ _ _ _

HUE OFTEN ASSOCIATED WITH ROSES   _ _ _

TO MAKE SOMEONE A PRIEST   _ _ _ _ _ _

AN OBJECT WHICH SEPARATES   _ _ _ _ _ _ _

◆?◆ ANSWER NO. 156 ◆?◆

LEVEL D

PUZZLE 121

Here are 40 sets of three letters. Using each set only once
and without changing the order of the letters
can you make 20 six-letter English words?

ora	can	joc	bas	mis	ver	plu	hap	ous	dam
gin	sen	fix	nor	ius	por	law	cud	wig	age
pen	out	suf	fam	qua	ear	ket	ral	try	key
mal	dle	ang	sel	voy	lay	gen	did	ter	mar

◆?◆ ANSWER NO. 48 ◆?◆

197

PUZZLE 122

Each line in the rhyme below gives one letter of a well-known city.
Can you work out the identity of this ten-letter European capital?

My first is in TRACE, but not in PLAN

My second's in ROTTEN, but not in MILAN

My third is in PORTRAIT, but not in SUNRISE

My fourth is in PRETTY, and also SURPRISE

My fifth is in FRIEND, but not in COMPARE

My sixth is in GHETTO, but not in DESPAIR

My seventh's in DECADE, and also in DAMP

My eighth is in GINGER, but not in REVAMP

My ninth is in GOVERN, and also in NIECE

My tenth is in LANGUAGE, but is not in CEASE.

 ANSWER NO.57

PUZZLE 123

How may words of three letters or more can you find in this square?
The computer found 102, but as you don't have a microchip in your head we don't expect you to get quite so many! A score of fifteen is good, twenty-five very good and forty or more excellent. What is the nine letter word?

 ANSWER NO.87

PUZZLE 124

Which of the following can be seen at some time in the night sky,
with a telescope if necessary?

URSA MAJOR BETELGEUSE

ORION COPERNICUS

CUMULUS ANTARCTICA

HORSE NEBULA PLUTO

JOHN MAJOR CASCARA

NEPTUNE PERSEIDS

VENUS HALLEY'S COMET

HADES DOMESTICA

?> ANSWER NO.110 <?

LEVEL D

PUZZLE 125

Below you'll find some anagrams of well-known people.
Can you work out who they are?

1. **G's huge bore** (American politician)

2. **C Kindles Search** (English writer)

3. **Moodier Me** (Actress)

4. **Shy without neon** (Singer)

5. **A new antic – So?** (Inventor)

?> ANSWER NO.12 <?

PUZZLE 126

Take a letter from each country in turn to make another 7 letter country.
Clue: It could feel a little chilly here!

```
I  R  E  L  A  N  D

A  M  E  R  I  C  A

G  E  R  M  A  N  Y

F  I  N  L  A  N  D

A  U  S  T  R  I  A

D  E  N  M  A  R  K

E  N  G  L  A  N  D
```

ANSWER NO.105

PUZZLE 127

Look carefully at the following 'words'. If you replace the numbers with
Roman numerals you should be able to read them easily.

1000 o 500 1 100 u 1000

100 a 500 1000 1 u 1000

a 100 a 500 e 1000 1 100

500 u 1000 1000 1 e 500

a 100 100 e 500 e 500

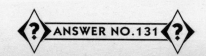

ANSWER NO.131

PUZZLE 128

Reading down, the name of a well-known young actress should be revealed in the middle column which is currently empty. To discover her identity, it is useful for you to know that each letter of her name will help you create two brand new words on every line, the left one ending with the letter, the right one starting. Who is she?

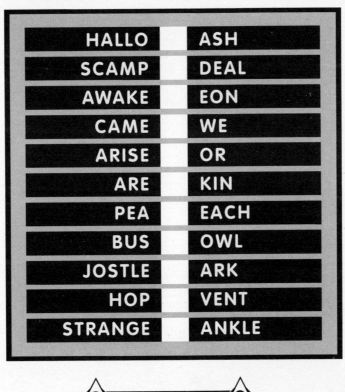

HALLO		ASH
SCAMP		DEAL
AWAKE		EON
CAME		WE
ARISE		OR
ARE		KIN
PEA		EACH
BUS		OWL
JOSTLE		ARK
HOP		VENT
STRANGE		ANKLE

? ANSWER NO.30 ?

LEVEL D

PUZZLE 129

The jumble of letters below contains five three-letter words. Each is the name of a living creature. The letters are in different type styles but always in the same order. The order is:

A B C

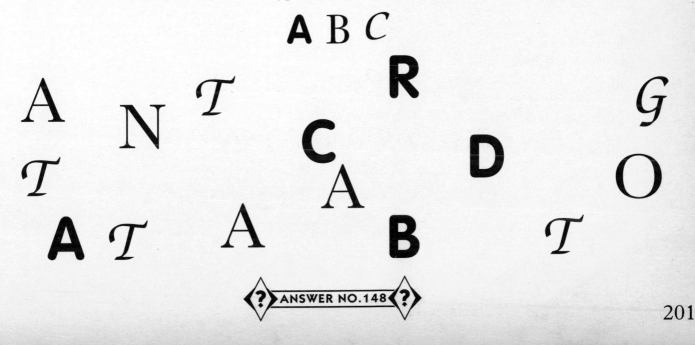

? ANSWER NO.148 ?

201

PUZZLE 130

There are five five-letter words hidden in the light bulbs.
Take a letter from each bulb to find them.
They have all something to do with light.

ANSWER NO.161

PUZZLE 131

If you cut letters in half horizontally it is much easier to recognise the top half than the bottom. For that reason all the words below are made up from – you guessed! – bottom halves. To help you, all the words are types of food.

ANSWER NO.21

PUZZLE 132

The names of two animals are hidden in each of the sentences below.
Can you find them?

1. A dynamo used by a mad scientist will endanger billionaires.

2. On her job application form she epitomised all the qualities they required.

3. Noah's tendency to cherish arks was perfectly understandable.

4. William wants to grab bits of gossip like him, do you abhor secrecy.

5. Peering through the uncommon keyhole he learnt of plans of their brilliant elopement.

6. He would like to go to Moscow but she insists on Budapest.

7. His bravado gave us a false impression: indeed the whole thing's a sham, sternness being our best reaction.

8. I prefer athletics, although the commentator's waffle annoys me.

ANSWER NO.39

PUZZLE 133

Below you can see a number of syllables in alphabetical order and a list of clues. All the answers to the clues can be made from combinations of the syllables given. Each syllable is used ONCE only. When you have solved all the clues, the first letters should give you the name of a well-known fictional character.

A   AL   AP   BRA   DI   DOUG   EM   GE   GO   IN   IT
JE   LA   LAS   LE   LEM   LY   MARE   MI   NA   NEP   NIGHT
ON   OR   OS   PER   PLE   PO   RU   SA   SA   TRICH   TUNE

CLUES

EUROPEAN COUNTRY (5)	FRUIT (5)	FLIGHTLESS BIRD (7)
FRENCH EMPEROR (8)	DREAM (9)	PLANET (7)
BOY'S NAME (6)	BRANCH OF MATHEMATICS (7)	SUPREME RULER (7)
COLOUR OF THE RAINBOW (6)	HOLY CITY (9)	SAUSAGE (6)

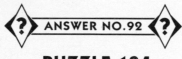 ANSWER NO.92

PUZZLE 134

The grid contains some letters to help you. Use the clues to fill in the missing letters and you will find a word written along the body of the snake.

Go up

Fight

Middle East

Saucy

Metal

Large birds of prey

Frozen north

Branches

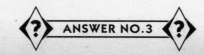 ANSWER NO.3

PUZZLE 135

The leaves of the tree contain groups of letters which, when unscrambled, will give you the names of five types of tree. What are they?

ANSWER NO. 118

PUZZLE 136

Look at the words on this moon map.
They form an anagram of a well known lunar feature.

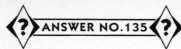

PUZZLE 137

Danny Diablo has gone on a school outing to the art gallery. His teacher prayed that, for once, he would be good but within minutes of entering the building he has switched round the names of several famous artists. Can you rearrange them before the warder notices and throws the whole class out?

206

PUZZLE 138

The words below have some of their letters replaced by symbols. Each symbol always represents the same letter. To help you we have also put in some clues.

Symbols	Clue
	Trading before money
	Party wind bag
	Make
	Dealer
	Plunderer
	Scold harshly

ANSWER NO.70

PUZZLE 139

In each sentence you'll find the name of one sport hidden.
Can you locate all six of them?

1. The whole thing was rather a shock, eyebrows being raised in the highest of places.

2. The English aristocracy clings to old values, for it fears a world without them.

3. That really was a bad mint on the whole; it stuck to my teeth like glue.

4. Her horrid ingratitude was beyond belief, and she was sent to bed without supper.

5. My cat will attack a rat every time.

6. He started making loud jokes in order to mask a tingling in his left foot.

ANSWER NO.157

PUZZLE 140

Along the arms of the tentacles of the octopus you will see the names
of marine creatures disguised in a special way. How many can you catch?

ANSWER NO.47

TEETH GRINDERS

★ LEVEL E ★

PUZZLE 141

The seven letter words below are all in code. The same symbol always stands for the same letter. To help you a clue is given at the end of each line and two letters have been left uncoded.

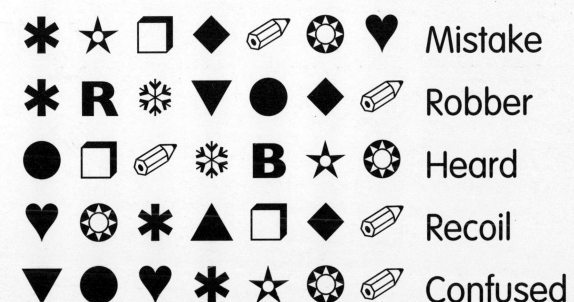

Mistake

Robber

Heard

Recoil

Confused

ANSWER NO.56

209

The following sentence is missing three words which are anagrams of each other. Each dash represents a missing letter. What are the words?

The _ _ _ _ _ _ _ said that I was a _ _ _ _ _ _ _ because I had the word _ _ _ _ _ _ _ written on my hand in the spelling test.

 ANSWER NO.88

TEETH GRINDERS

PUZZLE 143

The answers to the clues below can be found in the list of syllables. However, all the syllables have been presented in alphabetical order. See if you can rearrange them.

BI CATH CLE COM CY ED FISH GA GOLD MA
NAI OS PIZ PU RAL SI TER TRICH ZA ZINE

CLUES

1. INFORMATION PROCESSOR
2. WILDERNESS AREA SOUTH OF ISRAEL
3. LARGE CHURCH
4. ITALIAN OPEN PIE
5. AQUATIC PET
6. LARGE FLIGHTLESS BIRD
7. PERIODICAL
8. CONVEYANCE

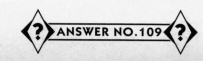 ANSWER NO.109

PUZZLE 144

The following eight-letter words have been coded using Greek style letters.
Even if you don't know any Greek you will be able to work out the words
if you use the clues we have given.

ΛΞΦΓΛΜΕΤ   HANDBONES

ΔΦΓΛΜΙΞΗ   BABY DUCK

ΙΞΛΜΙΞΗΤ   VAGUE IDEAS

ΠΙΓΛΜΙΞΗ   PRESERVING FOOD

ΙΞΓΜΦΔΕΤ   CONTAINS

? ANSWER NO.11 ?

PUZZLE 145

The following sentences have been de-punctuated to turn them into nonsense.
Can you add punctuation to make them grammatical?
Each is not necessarily a single sentence.

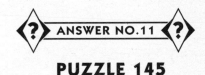

1. She said that that that that I said should have been those

2. The culprit made his admission sorrowfully the day after he was shot

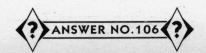

3. I said and but he said I said but but he was wrong and I said so

? ANSWER NO.106 ?

LEVEL E

211

PUZZLE 146

The words in the box have something in common.
Which of the following words should join them?

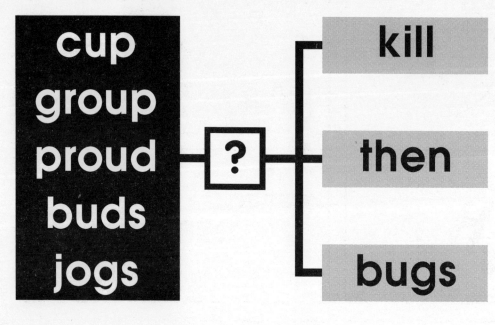

cup
group
proud
buds
jogs

?

kill

then

bugs

?ANSWER NO.132?

PUZZLE 147

The following groups of words are all proverbs in which the words
have been jumbled up. How many can you work out?

1 And many between cup there's slip a lip

2 They count before your hatch chickens don't

3 Judge cover by its never a book

4 Most vessels make empty noise

5 Be out find your sure sin will you

?ANSWER NO.29?

PUZZLE 148

A rebus is a word, phrase or saying cunningly hidden in a illustration.

Here are a few to try.

1. JUST

2. c l o u d

3. IS (bell)

4. S H I P

5. THING THING

6. STEP STEP

7. VIOLINIST

8. THE
RESORT
RESORT
RESORT
RESORT

9. **PIGGY**
PIGGY
PIGGY

10. WHECAS ƧᴙIꞀAZ TAWLUN CANPE

11. YOUNG

12. S E A L

13. ROOST (ruler 1-12)

ANSWER NO.149

LEVEL E

PUZZLE 149

The answers to the clues below are syllables which, when rearranged,
will make the names of five countries. To help you,
there's a hint to the identity of the syllables in brackets after each clue.

A stain or blot (rhymes with 'spark')   **The first letter of the alphabet**

Me (rhymes with 'pie')   (rhymes with 'pay')

An old fashioned girl's name   **Some** (rhymes with 'penny')

(rhymes with 'wader')   **Part of the face** (rhymes with 'bin')

Home of a predatory animal   **A tin for food** (rhymes with 'man')

(rhymes with 'when')   **Past tense of run** (rhymes with 'fan')

Common name for the thing which causes illness (rhymes with 'worm')

 ANSWER NO.160

PUZZLE 150

Can you fill in these blanks? In each puzzle the letters
missing are the same for every line.

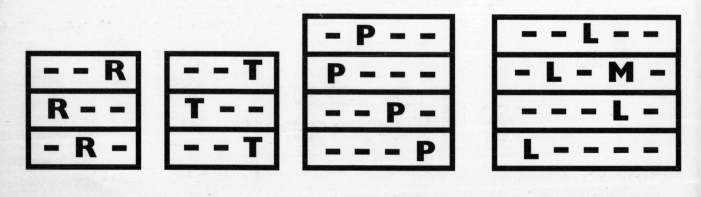

ANSWER NO.20

PUZZLE 151

Using the letters we have given you and the clues on the right fill in the missing letters. When you have finished you will find there is a word running down the snake.

Finger

Thousands of Years

Desert plants

Hit

Tree Seed

Pains

Another name

Happiness

Greek Island

ANSWER NO.38

ANSWER NO.38

PUZZLE 152

Can you unravel these ten words? The clues in brackets could help you, as they mean the same as the scrambled words.

1. **EITDRVNE**
(back to front)

2. **DAEOFHLSO**
(lie)

3. **VLICARUSHO**
(gallant)

4. **ASDEHFMI**
(starving)

5. **HIANVS**
(disappear)

6. **REOMET**
(shooting star)

7. **LHEROCT**
(laugh)

8. **UPSSEO**
(husband)

9. **CARCIEP**
(whim)

10. **ETRPMEITD**
(allowed)

ANSWER NO.73

LEVEL E

PUZZLE 153

The words in the box have been chosen according to a simple system.
Can any of the words outside join them.

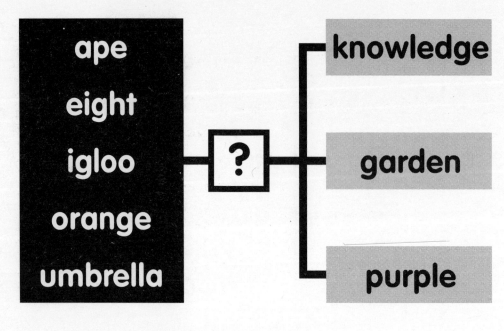

ape
eight
igloo
orange
umbrella

?

knowledge

garden

purple

? ANSWER NO.91 **?**

PUZZLE 154

In each of the five sentences below two numbers are hiding.
It is your task to seek them out.

1. Bridget went yesterday, anxious even though we had reassured her she would be alright.

2. At the windmill I once played my accordion every day.

3. Keith reeled in surprise as the horse's sudden neigh threw him into confusion.

4. He was left woefully short of cash, having been spending again in excess of what he could truly afford.

5. The scheme was foolproof, our accountant encouraged us to start immediately.

? ANSWER NO.2 **?**

PUZZLE 155

Use the clues to fill in the missing words and complete the snail. To help you you'll find that the last letter of each word must be used as the first letter of the next word. The number of letters for each answer is given at the end of the clue.

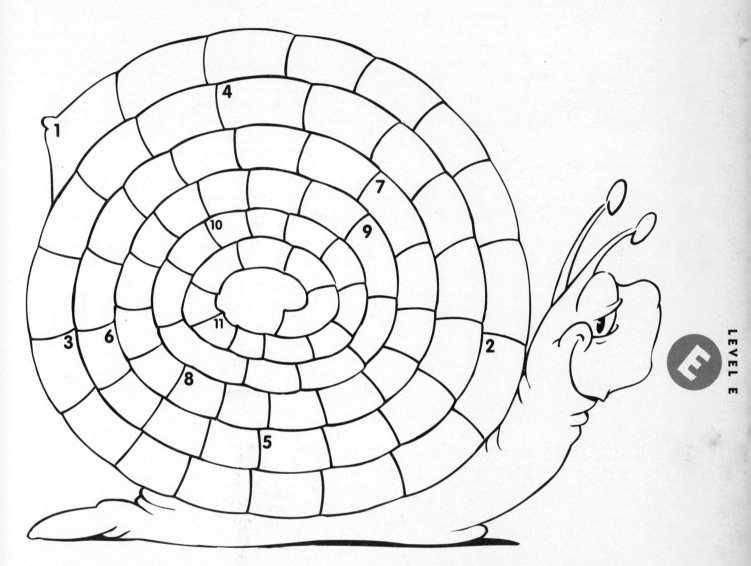

1. Pay this in class or teacher won't be pleased (9)

2. This is most of the air we breath (8)

3. Lump of gold (6)

4. You can bear it – just about! (9)

5. Weird (5)

6. Aubergine (8)

7. The hare will always beat him in the race (8)

8. The person who saw the crime (10)

9. A noisy quarrel (8)

10. Getting the chop at dawn! (9)

11. Zero (7)

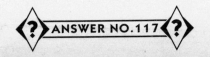 ANSWER NO.117

PUZZLE 156

Take a letter from each animal and make five
six-letter words connected with farms.

1

ANSWER NO. 134

PUZZLE 157

Here we have mixed the names of trees with the names of places where people live. See if you can untangle the resulting strange words.

PALBEAM

HORNACE   CAPLE   MASTLE

GALOWRED

BUNWOOD

MONAR

HICKAGE

COTTORY

CEDASTERY

 **ANSWER NO. 175**

PUZZLE 158

The words around the circle can be rearranged to form the name of a country.
Clue: 51

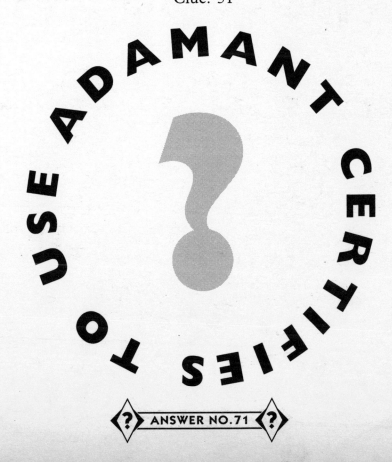

ADAMANT CERTIFIES TO USE

ANSWER NO. 71

219

PUZZLE 159

Complete the phrases below, then write the missing words in the grid
with the first letter in the box. You should be able to read a six-letter word down.

Clue: Fish

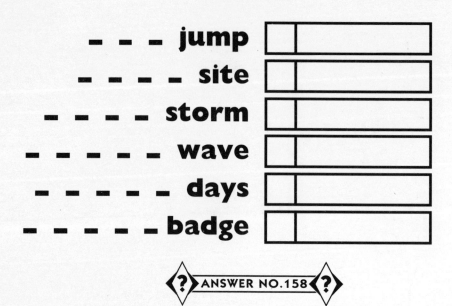

- - - jump

- - - - site

- - - - storm

- - - - - wave

- - - - - days

- - - - - badge

?ANSWER NO.158?

PUZZLE 160

Change the top word into the bottom one by altering a letter each time
and forming a new word with each move.

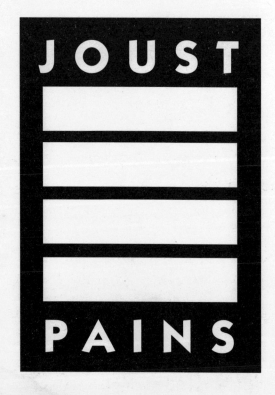

?ANSWER NO.46?

220

PUZZLE 161

Match the following words with their position on the body shown.

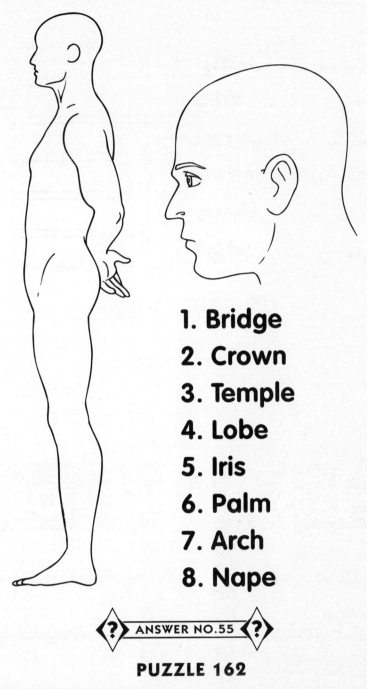

1. **Bridge**
2. **Crown**
3. **Temple**
4. **Lobe**
5. **Iris**
6. **Palm**
7. **Arch**
8. **Nape**

ANSWER NO.55

PUZZLE 162

Below you will see thirty syllables. If you rearrange them you'll find that, using each syllable only once, they will make up ten three-syllable words. What are the words?

DI	MAN	TEER	PA	SUS	TUDE	GAST	IN	REAU	DO
SION	AB	NANCE	VER	PER	CATE	GI	BU	BER	UN
TIC	NEWS	LON	DI	RO	VOL	FLAB	MEN	CRAT	TE

ANSWER NO.89

221

PUZZLE 163

Use all the letters in the grid twice to give you two nine-letter words.
The clue is: SILENT LADY KILLERS

◇?◇ ANSWER NO.108 ◇?◇

PUZZLE 164

The following clues will give you the name of six sports.
Read the first letters of the words in order
and you will be transported to Africa.

Natation	
Toxophily	
Soccer	
Track & Field	
Equestrianism	
Blade Balance	

◇?◇ ANSWER NO.10 ◇?◇

PUZZLE 165

Which of the words in the right-hand column can join the left?

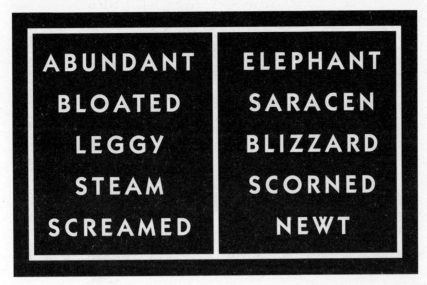

ABUNDANT	ELEPHANT
BLOATED	SARACEN
LEGGY	BLIZZARD
STEAM	SCORNED
SCREAMED	NEWT

ANSWER NO.107

PUZZLE 166

Below you will find some clues. We have given you the answers as well!
So where's the puzzle? Well, the answers have been broken into syllables arranged
in alphabetical order. All you have to do is select the right syllables to
answer each clue. Easy! Or is it?

1. AMERICAN UNIVERSITY

2. CAPITAL OF THAILAND

3. COMMON NAME OF PLANT RANUNCULUS

4. ANIMAL WHICH CARRIES ITS YOUNG IN A POUCH

5. GAMBLING GAME INVOLVING WHEEL

6. VERY HARD CRYSTALLINE CARBON

7. TREES WHICH LOOSE THEIR LEAVES IN WINTER

8. CALEDONIA

9. EATER OF ITS OWN KIND

10. PART OF OUR GALAXY

LEVEL E

A	AL	BANG	BUT	CAN	CUP	DEC	DI	ET
HAR	IAL	ID	KOK	LAND	LETTE	MAR	MOND	NIB
OUS	PLAN	ROU	SCOT	SUP	TER	U	VARD	

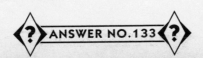
ANSWER NO.133

223

AAARGH!

★ **LEVEL F** ★

PUZZLE 167

The letters below can be fitted into the grid so that they give three words reading across and one down the middle.

PBTTFAYCUSDEANRA

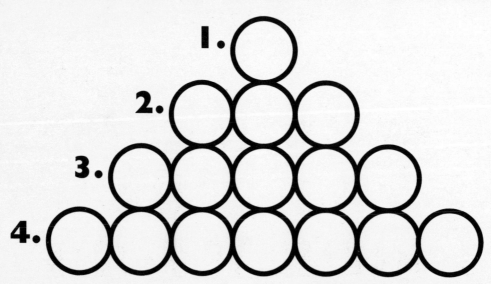

1. **Single letter vegetable**

3. **Well again**

2. **Nocturnal flying animal**

4. **Imagination**

ANSWER NO.28

PUZZLE 168

Five of the words below are related in some way. Discover which ones they are and see if brass could join them.

hares cease
beach sloth
brown again
frown abbey
beans green
drama acids

 ANSWER NO.193

PUZZLE 169

Turn the anagrams below into four classic works of English literature. Name the authors too. Clue: there is a hint to the theme of the books in the anagram.

1. MASK PLAN FIRED

2. SITED HARM

3. MAULED TO REJOIN

4. BOSS DEFILER V THE LUSTRE

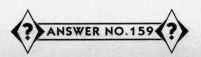 ANSWER NO.159

PUZZLE 170

Look at the following list of words. There is something special about them.
Can you work out what it is?

HOAX   **THAW**   **AVOW**

IOTA   **ATOM**   **TAXI**

MIAOW

? ANSWER NO.192 ?

PUZZLE 171

Look at the signpost below. The distances given are related, by some form
of twisted logic, to the place names. Can you work out the logic and then replace the
question mark with the correct distance? If you want a clue, remember the words
have consonants and vowels.

AAARGH! **F**

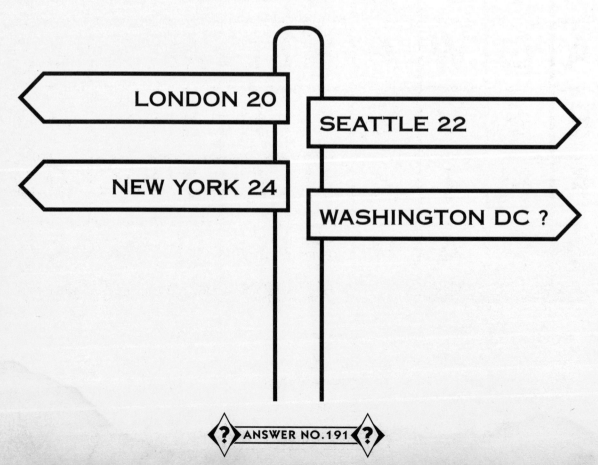

LONDON 20

SEATTLE 22

NEW YORK 24

WASHINGTON DC ?

? ANSWER NO.191 ?

PUZZLE 172

The clues will help you to find ten hidden words all to do with cycling. The words may be written in any direction and the grid contains dummy letters.

A	X	M	I	R	R	O	R	O	R	H
B	E	L	D	D	A	S	B	A		
W	I	L	R	T	V	E	S	N		
P	O	C	E	T	L	S	E	D		
E	E	U	Y	L	J	B	K	L		
M	E	D	S	C	A	L	O	E		
A	G	W	A	N	L	M	P	B		
R	E	V	Q	L	R	E	S	A		
F	N	I	A	H	C	T	Y	R		
D	R	A	U	G	D	U	M	S		

LEVEL F

1. Reflector	**5.** Driver	**8.** Ringer
2. Steering device	**6.** Splash	**9.** Bike
3. Wheel parts	preventor	**10.** Skeleton
4. Foot rest	**7.** Seat	

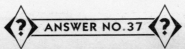

PUZZLE 173

ACROSS

1. Tall pole on a ship which supports the sail (4)
6. A person who has no parents (6)
8. Father (2)
9. Part of something (4)
10. It helps you to draw straight lines (5)
12. Tea, lemonade and orange juice are these (6)
13. To carry out something (2)
14. This would be steep to walk up (6)
16. A male deer (4)
18. You use this on your hair to make it stay in place (3)
19. A baby horse (4)
21. You open and close this (4)
23. A narrow passageway (8)

DOWN

1. The early part of the day (7)
2. I am, you _ _ _ (3)
3. A flash (5)
4. A type of bird (6)
5. An outlaw (6)
7. You use this to mend your clothes (6)
11. You fasten this in your hair to make it curl (6)
15. An eskimo's home (5)
16. Water in a plant (3)
17. As well (4)
19. A long way (3)
20. To unite by addition (3)
22. Either, _ _ (2)

ANSWER NO. 72

The letters on the computer screen form a series. What letter replaces the question mark?

OTTFF SSEN?

? ANSWER NO.90 ?

PUZZLE 175

Can you work out where these people live?

Fit the names correctly into the boxes and you should have your answer!

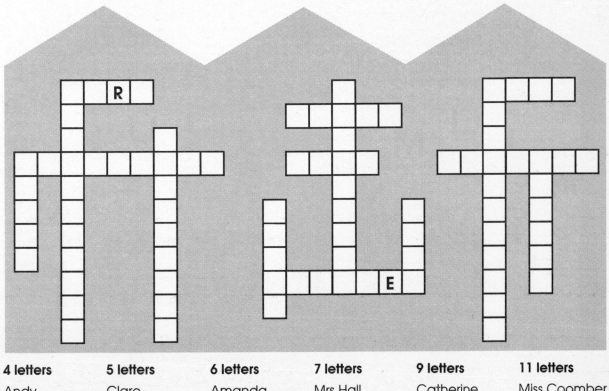

LEVEL F

4 letters	5 letters	6 letters	7 letters	9 letters	11 letters
Andy	Clare	Amanda	Mrs Hall	Catherine	Miss Coomber
Mary	Sarah		Shelley	Miss Cooke	Mrs Tuckwell
Mike	Tessa			Mr Bushell	
Paul					

? ANSWER NO.1 ?

229

PUZZLE 176

Five of the words below are related. Discover which ones they are
and then see if confidence could join them.

encyclopedia

anteater

ahead

astrology

red

confederation

hopeless

acrimony

eagles

nausea

acids

telephone

sight

azalea

 ANSWER NO.190

AAARGH!

PUZZLE 177

The editor's going to be after me. A number puzzle in a word puzzle book!
Whatever next? But no, I assure you this is a word puzzle.
Why are some numbers above the line?

12   6   10

345   789

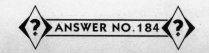 ANSWER NO.184

PUZZLE 178

Start at the top left corner and fill in the answers to the clues, working round the grid in a spiral. The last two letters of each answer form the first two of the next. The number of letters in each answer is given in brackets after the clue.

LEVEL F

1. Capital of UK (6)
2. Vegetable (5)
3. One time only (4)
4. Stop completely (5)
5. Quite a few (7)
6. Permit (5)
7. Possessor (5)
8. Rub out (5)
9. Older (6)
10. Command (5)
11. Historical periods (4)
12. Study of the stars (9)
13. Gold, Frankincense and – – – – – (5)
14. Words with similar endings (eg. Prime time) (5)
15. Given by the Doctor (8)
16. Uneasy (7)
17. Everyday (5)
18. Boy with magic lamp (7)
19. Not seen (9)
20. Citrus fruit (5)
21. Single unit (3)
22. More recent (5)
23. Wipe out completely (9)
24. Extreme fear (6)
25. Groups of fruit trees (8)

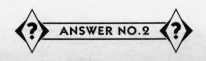

ANSWER NO.2

PUZZLE 179

Your task here is to work out which letter of the alphabet is represented by each of the numbers 1 to 26. To help you, we've given you a few letters to start you off. When you work out what the numbers represent, write them in the reference grid at the bottom. The completed puzzle will look like a filled-in crossword, featuring only genuine words.

AAARGH!

		8			22	16	10	6	4	7	4	3
25	8	11	11	6		8		16		21	7	
7		7		16		10			14		21	11
26	7	4	21		1		22	24	15	11		23
7			7		4	11			7			9
4			18	16	16		9	6	22	5		6
9	20	24	11		26				13	9	6	
	11			10	9	2	5	6		12		16
	8		2	7	6	11			17	11	7	20
			21		10	7	9	24				20
7	4	6		11		6			15		9	
	7		16			24		12	11	25	6	
	19	15	10	2	24	11				16		

1	2	3	4	5	6	7	8	9	10	11	12	13
			R		T		W		N	E		
14	15	16	17	18	19	20	21	22	23	24	25	26
		O								L		

ANSWER NO.76

232

PUZZLE 180

Look at the diagrams, crack the logic of the puzzle, and discover the missing letters.

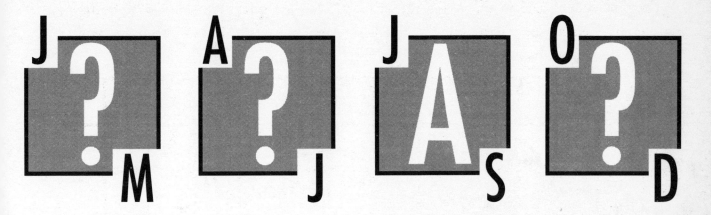

ANSWER NO.188

PUZZLE 181

Here is part of the menu from Joe's Diner. Joe has his own way of calculating the prices. We're not giving away too many secrets if we tell you it has someting to do with the position of letters in the alphabet. How much does Pizza cost? If you can work it out Joe will give you a free slice.

Joe's Diner

Hamburger
...... $9.30

Cheeseburger $11.60

Hot Dog
...... $6.90

Pizza
...... ?

ANSWER NO.189

PUZZLE 182

In the diagram you see the magic word Abracadabra spelt out as a pyramid. There are various paths from top to bottom but how many ways can you discover to spell the trick word?

A
B B
R R R
A A A A
C C C C C
A A A A A A
D D D D D D D
A A A A A A A A
B B B B B B B B B
R R R R R R R R R R
A A A A A A A A A A A

ANSWER NO.187

PUZZLE 183

Start at the top left square and fill in the answers to the clues.
The LAST TWO letters of each word form the first two letters of the next word.
Follow the grid in an ever-decreasing spiral to the centre.

1. Wild dog (6)

2. Water tortoise (8)

3. Discoverer of new ideas (8)

4. Musical instrument (5)

5. Story (8)

6. Used for long distance conversation (9)

7. Worn for decoration (8)

8. Eaten at breakfast (6)

9. Type of maths (7)

10. Demanded by kidnappers (6)

11. Sign to the superstitious (4)

12. Holds a letter (8)

13. Fruit (4)

14. Reach your destination (6)

15. Pest (6)

16. Crazy (6)

17. Closer (6)

18. Mistake (5)

19. Music makers (10)

20. To do with fortune telling using the stars (12)

ANSWER NO.19

235

PUZZLE 184

Just a brief message, irritatingly obscure of course.
Can you work it out?

FYTHNKTHSSGNGTBS
YYHDBTTRTHNKAGN

 ANSWER NO.183

PUZZLE 185

Look at the signpost below. The distances given are related, by some form of twisted logic, to the place names. Can you work out the logic and then replace the question mark with the correct distance?

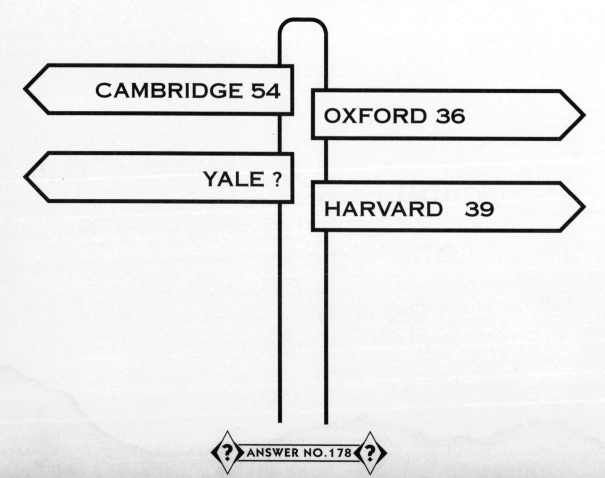

CAMBRIDGE 54

OXFORD 36

YALE ?

HARVARD 39

PUZZLE 186

The letters in the computer screen make a series.
Work out the logic and replace the question mark.

AEAPAU
UUECO?

 ANSWER NO.150

PUZZLE 187

Five of the words below are related. Discover which ones they are
and then see if heady could join them.

fireball

ready

it

yellow

transubstantiation

hamburger

analysis

anything

bottomless

acolyte

rival

rivet

golf

 ANSWER NO.185

PUZZLE 188

Look at the word below. It's actually Monrovian for 'Mine's a large cheeseburger with extra relish.' No, that's a lie. But the letters do have one strange property. What is it?

EHIKOX

 ANSWER NO. 186

PUZZLE 189

Five of the words below are related. Discover which ones they are and then see if ability could join them.

AAARGH!

ziggurat average

gizmo

ear

introduction

onomatopoeia

xylophone

uncle

classic

hangman

numerical

depend force

grass white

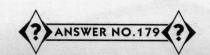 ANSWER NO. 179

238

PUZZLE 190

Look at the signpost below. The distances given are related, by some form of twisted logic, to the place names. Can you work out the logic and then replace the question mark with the correct distance?

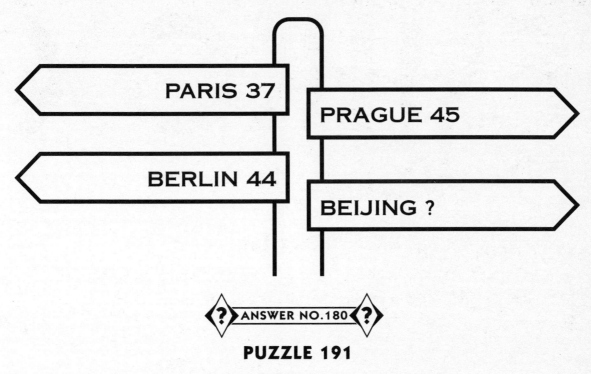

PARIS 37

PRAGUE 45

BERLIN 44

BEIJING ?

?◆ ANSWER NO.180 ◆?

PUZZLE 191

Too many people knew the code to Joe's menu and he was losing a fortune in free pizza. Now he has a new code (still based on the value of letters). Can you crack it, discover the price of pancakes, and win a free hamburger?

Joe's Diner

Apple Pie $13.60
Icecream $15.90
Chocolate Cake....$24.90
Pancakes .... ?

?◆ ANSWER NO.182 ◆?

PUZZLE 192

Look at the signpost below. The distances given are related, by some form of twisted logic, to the place names. Can you work out the logic and then replace the question mark with the correct distance? If you want a clue, remember that words have consonants and vowels.

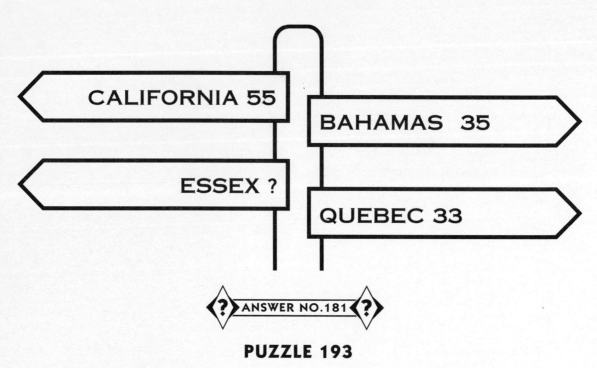

CALIFORNIA 55

BAHAMAS 35

ESSEX ?

QUEBEC 33

ANSWER NO.181

PUZZLE 193

Walter is planning a holiday but is not quite sure where he's going. Can you help him by matching the country to the capital city.

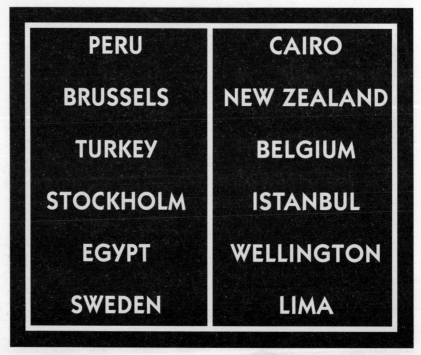

PERU	CAIRO
BRUSSELS	NEW ZEALAND
TURKEY	BELGIUM
STOCKHOLM	ISTANBUL
EGYPT	WELLINGTON
SWEDEN	LIMA

ANSWER NO.74

AAARGH!

ANSWERS

1

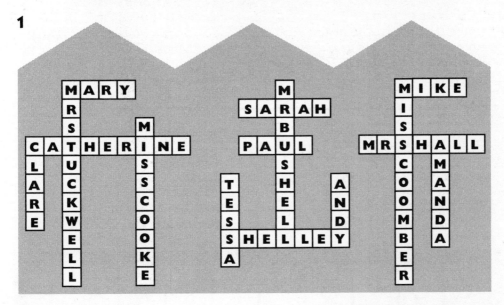

2
1. London.
2. Onion.
3. Once.
4. Cease.
5. Several.
6. Allow
7. Owner.
8. Erase.
9. Senior.
10. Order.
11. Era.
12. Astronomy.
13. Myrrh.
14. Rhyme.
15. Medicine.
16. Nervous.
17. Usual.
18. Aladdin.
19. Invisible.
20. Lemon.
21. One.
22. Newer.
23. Eradicate.
24. Terror.
25. Orchards.

3 Ascend, Battle, Arabia, Cheeky, Bronze, Eagles, Arctic, Boughs.
The answer is Strength.

4 Creep, Alibi, Nails, Comic, Eagle, Rails.
The signs of the zodiac are Cancer and Pisces.

5 Cinderella.

6 Indigo, Number, Treaty, Race, India, Glue, Umbrella, Elephant.
The word is intrigue.

7 John Lennon
Helena Bonham-Carter
Napoleon Bonaparte
Elizabeth Taylor
Neil Armstrong
Albert Einstein
Richard Gere.

8 Horse, Goats, Mules, Sheep, Ducks.

9 Red.

10 Swimming, Archery, Football, Athletics, Riding, Ice skating.
The word is Safari.

241

11 Knuckles, Ducklings, Inklings, Pickling, Includes.

12 George Bush
Charles Dickens
Demi Moore
Whitney Houston
Isaac Newton.

13 Too many cooks spoil the broth.
A stich in time saves nine.
It never rains but it pours.
Rome wasn't built in a day.
Birds of a feather flock together.

14 Little Red Riding Hood.

15 Sonic the Hedgehog.

16 Smell, Maid, Cheap, Thank, Peace, Flog, Weld, Beard.
The girl's name is Michelle.

17 Arm, Head, Leg, Foot.

18 Lucy. (Captain Hook, Peter Pan, Christopher Robin, Humpty Dumpty, Mother Goose, Betty Botter).

19 See below.

20 1. Mar, Ram, Arm.
2. Art, Tar, Rat.
3. Spar, Pars, Raps, Rasp.
4. Miles, Slime, Smile, Limes.

21 Pizza, Chicken, Doughnut, Sandwich, Salad, Ice cream.

22 Dog, Goldfish, Rabbit.

23 Faint heart never won fair lady.
A bird in the hand is worth two in the bush.
Its no use crying over spilt milk.

ANSWERS

19

C	O	Y	O	T	E	R	R	A	P
K	L	A	C	E	R	E	A	L	I
C	R	I	V	E	R	M	I	G	N
E	R	H	E	S	T	R	N	E	V
N	A	C	G	I	C	A	S	B	E
O	E	R	O	L	A	S	A	R	N
H	P	O	L	O	R	T	N	A	T
P	O	R	R	E	R	A	E	N	O
E	L	E	V	N	E	M	O	S	R
L	E	T	O	D	C	E	N	A	G

242

People who live in glass houses shouldn't throw stones.

24 Fast, Area, Sets, Task.

25 Become. The words start and end with consecutive letters of the alphabet, eg, AdverB, CarD, EngulF, etc.

26 Kirsty. It doesn't have the letter A in it.

27 Apes.

28

```
            P
      B A T
  C   U R E D
F A N T A S Y
```

29 There's many a slip between cup and lip.
Don't count your chickens before they hatch.
Never judge a book by it's cover.
Empty vessels make most noise.
Be sure your sin will find you out.

30 Winona Ryder.

31 Tyrannosaurus Rex.

32 Eggs, as all the others are dairy products.
August, as all the others have an 'R' in the month.
Spider, as all the others are insects.
Poland, as all the others are in the European Union.
Nova Scotia, as all the others are in America.
Harley-Davidson, as all the others are cars.
Cambridge, as all the others are rivers.
Cyclone, as all the others are types of cloud.

33 Apple, Norman, Opera, Night, Yellow Mark, Opium, Ugly, Sea.
The word is anonymous.

34 Neigh, Snowy, Ready Thorn, Large.

35 Bulldog, Dogfish.

36 Father Christmas.

37 See over.

38 Digit, Aeons, Cacti, Knock, Acorn, Aches, Alias, Bliss, Crete
The answer is deckchair.

39 1. Mouse and Gerbil.
2. Cat and Sheep.
3. Shark and Wasp.
4. Rabbit and Horse.
5. Monkey and Antelope.
6. Cow and Ape.
7. Dog and Hamster.
8. Rat and Flea.

40 Rota, Nostril, Lair, Joust.
The 10 letter word is journalist.

41 Rumplestiltskin.

42 25.

43 Oliver Cromwell
Mahatma Gandhi
George Washington
William Cody
Michelle Pfeiffer
Julia Roberts
Robin Hood.

44 Catherine Wheel.

45 Unbearable.

46 Joust, Joist, Joint, Point, Paint, Pains.
Clock, Cloak, Croak, Creak, Break, Bread.

47 Catfish, Plaice, Marlin, Dolphin, Haddock, Tunny, Squid, Oyster. All vowels are replaced by X.

48 Angora
Basket
Candid
Cuddle
Damsel

A	X	M	I	R	R	O	R	H
A	B	E	L	D	D	A	S	B	A
W	I	L	R	T	V	E	S	N
P	R	O	C	E	T	L	S	E	D
E	E	U	Y	L	J	B	K	L
M	E	D	S	C	A	L	O	E
A	G	W	A	N	L	M	P	B
R	E	V	Q	L	R	E	S	A
F	N	I	A	H	C	T	Y	R
D	R	A	U	G	D	U	M	S

Earwig,
Famous
Genius
Happen,
Jockey
Margin
Mislay,
Normal
Outlaw
Porter
Plural
Quaver
Sentry
Suffix
Voyage.

49 Green Card
Gorillas in the Mist
Some Like it Hot

Who's That Girl?
Hannah and her Sisters
Mannequin
It's a Wonderful Life
Star Wars
Always
Little Women.

50 Chinese, Arabic, Italian,
English, Spanish.

51 And, Bat, Dad, Eat,
Bad, End.

52 Bare/Bear, Hare/Hair,
Hart/Heart, Deer/Dear,
Reed/Read, Beet/Beat.

53 Ran.

54 Pa, Pan, Pane, Panel.

55 See below.

56 Blunder, Brigand,
Audible, Rebound, Garbled.

57 Copenhagen.

58 The Once and
Future King.
The House at Pooh
Corner.
How does your
garden grow.
I'll huff and I'll puff.

59 Adhesive, Advise, Advises,
Ashes, Aside, Asides, Aide,
Aides, Aids, Avid, Dash,
Dashes, Dais, Daises,
Devise, Devises, Dies,
Dish, Dishes, Disease,
Diva, Divas, Dive, Dives,
Have, Haves, Head, Heads,
Heavies, Heave, Heaved,
Heaves, Heed, Heeds,
Hide, Hides, Hiss, Hissed,
Hive, Hies, Hived, Hives,
Ease, Eased, Eases, Eaves,
Evade, Evades, Eves, Said,
Save, Saved, Saves, Sash,
Shad, Shade, Shades,
Shads, Shave, Shaved,
Shaves, Sheave, Sheaved,
Sheaves, Shed, Sheds,
Shield, Shies, Seas, Seaside,
Seeds, Seeds, Sees, Side,
Sides, Sieve, Sieved, Sieves,
Idea, Ideas, Ides, Vase,
Vases, Vied, Vies, Visa,
Visas.

60 Portugal, Hungary,
Romania, Germany, Greece.

61 E.

62 Vermicelli. This is a food.

63 To be or not to be,
That is the question.
(The first and last
letters are removed).

64 Scatter.
65 S. (The first letter of

Monday, Tuesday, etc.)

66 Idaho.

67 Journey to the Centre
of the Earth.
The Last of the Mohicans.
Twenty Thousand Leagues
Under the Sea.
The Little House on
the Prairie.
On Her Majesty's
Secret Service.

55

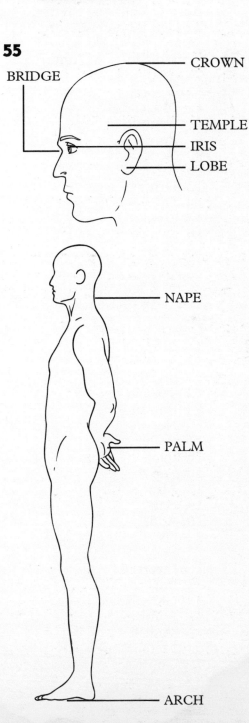

CROWN
BRIDGE
TEMPLE
IRIS
LOBE
NAPE
PALM
ARCH

68
1. Phantom of the Opera.
2. Carousel.
3. Evita.
4. Starlight Express.
5. The Sound of Music.
6. Les Miserables.
7. Chess.
8. Miss Saigon.
9. Rocky Horror Show.
10. Cats.

69 Acrobatic.

70 Barter, Balloon, Create, Trader, Looter, Berate.

71 United States of America.

72 Across
1. Mast
6. Orphan
8. Pa
9. Rear
10. Ruler
12. Drinks
13. Do
14. Hill
16. Stag
18. Gel
19. Foal
21. Door
23. Corridor.

Down
1. Morning
2. Are
3. Spark
4. Thrush
5. Bandit
7. Needle
11. Roller
15. Igloo
16. Sap
17. Also
19. Far
20. Add
22. Or.

73
1. Inverted
2. Falsehood
3. Chivalrous
4. Famished
5. Vanish
6. Meteor
7. Chortle
8. Spouse
9. Caprice
10. Permitted

74 Peru, Lima
New Zealand, Wellington
Belgium, Brussels
Turkey, Istanbul
Sweden, Stockholm
Egypt, Cairo.

75 Cormorant
Crow
Cuckoo
Chaffinch
Canary.

76 See next page.

77 Back.

78 Andre Agassi.

79 Aches.

80 The correct order is omen, pole, fork, knee.
The word is moon.

81 The correct order is shop, away need, down.
Sand is found on the beach.

82 Read down the eighth column from the left, the first letter is on the third line.

83 Settler, Letters.

84 Show and Sow
Open and Pen
Front and Font
Insane and Inane
Fear and Far
Cap and Carp
Neat and Net
Damp and Amp
Rain and Ran
Pest and Pet
Chop and Cop.
Sauce: Horseradish.

85 Money, Honey, Phoney, Phone, Home, Hole, Mole.

86
1. Alice in Wonderland.
2. Tom Sawyer.
3. Dracula.
4. Gulliver's Travels.
5. The Witches.

| P¹ | G² | Y³ | R⁴ | H⁵ | T⁶ | A⁷ | W⁸ | I⁹ | N¹⁰ | E¹¹ | V¹² | K¹³ |
| Q¹⁴ | U¹⁵ | O¹⁶ | B¹⁷ | Z¹⁸ | J¹⁹ | D²⁰ | M²¹ | C²² | X²³ | L²⁴ | S²⁵ | F²⁶ |

87 Bob, Bobs, Bobsleigh, Bosh, Bole, Boles, Boil, Boils, Bog, Bogs, Bogie, Bogies, Blob, Blobs, Beg, Begs, Bib, Bibs, Bible, Bibles, Bile, Bilge, Big, Oblige, Obliges, Obeli, Oil, Oils Ogle, Ogles, Ohs, Sob, Sol, Sole, Soli, Soil, Soh, Slob, Sloe, Slog, Sleigh, Silo, Sigh, Shoe She, Lob, Lobbies, Lobs, Lobe, Lobes, Lose, Log, Logs, Loge, Loges, Lei, Leis, Leg, Legs, Lib, Lie, Lies, Ebb, Ebbs, Ego, Egos, Isle, Gob, Gobs, Gobble, Gobbles, Goch, Goes, Glob, Globs, Globe, Globes, Glib, Gel, Gels, Gib, Gibboxe, Gibs, Gibe, Gibes, Hob, Hobble, Hobbles, Hobbies, Hobs, Hose, Hole, Holes, Holies, Hoe, Hoes, Hog, Hogs, His, Hie, Hies.

88 Teacher, Cheater, Hectare.

89 Abdomen, Bureaucrat, Diversion, Flabbergast, Indicate, Longitude, Newspaper, Romantic, Sustenance, Volunteer.

90 T. (The first letter of one, two three etc.)

91 No. The words in the box each begins with one of the vowels in their usual order.

92 Italy, Napoleon, Douglas, Indigo, Apple, Nightmare, Algebra, Jerusalem, Ostrich, Neptune, Emperor, Salami. The character is Indiana Jones.

93 California, Idaho Nebraska, Hawaii, Alaska.

94 Raiders of the Lost Ark.

95 Rain, Snow, Hail, Mist.

96 Spare
Pears
Reaps
Pares
Spear.

97 Rocking Horse.

98 Four, Seven, One, Six. When added together they make eighteen.

99 Sarah, Fiona, George, James.

100 Play time.

101 Earwig, Centipede, Tarantula, Cockroach, Earthworm.

102 See over.

103 Denmark, Canada, Germany, Ireland, New Zealand.

104 Robinson Crusoe
Swiss Family Robinson
The Three Musketeers
Tales of Tom Bombadil
The Chronicles of Narnia.

105 Iceland.

106 She said that that 'that' that I said should have been 'those.'

The culprit made his admission sorrowfully. The day after he was shot.

I said 'and' but he said I said 'but,' but he was wrong and I said so.

ANSWERS

107 Scorned. (All the words contain food.)

108 Noiseless Lionesses.

109 1. Computer.
2. Sinai.
3. Cathedral.
4. Pizza.
5. Goldfish.
6. Ostrich.
7. Magazine.
8. Bicycle.

110 Ursa Major
Orion
Horse Nebula
Neptune
Venus
Betelgeuse
Pluto
Perseids
Halley's Comet.

111 1. All that glitters (glisters) is not gold.
2. A rolling stone gathers no moss.
3. The grass is always greener on the other side of the fence.
4. Set a thief to catch a thief.
5. Troubles always seem to come in threes.

112 Butter
Totter
Barrel
Longer
Rubble
Totals.

113 Hand.

102

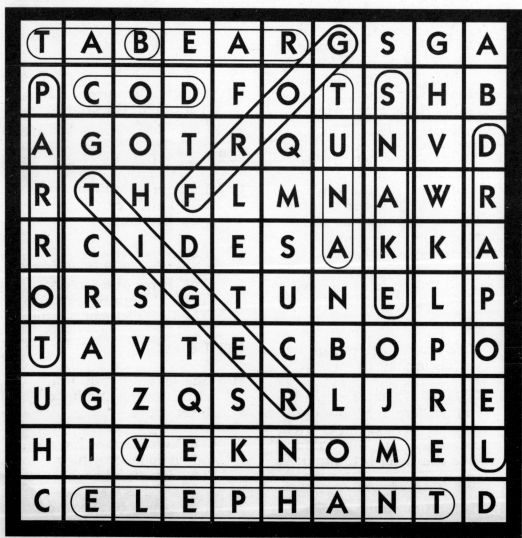

114 Accountant, Pilot, Teacher, Nurse, Discjockey.

115 Bedtime story.

116 Herd, Clutch, Gaggle, Pride, School.

117
1. Attention
2. Nitrogen
3. Nugget
4. Tolerable
5. Eerie
6. Eggplant
7. Tortoise
8. Eyewitness
9. Squabble
10. Execution
11. Nothing.

118 Chestnut
Lime
Redwood
Laburnum
Douglas Fir

119 Catapult. (All the words include the name of an animal.)

120 Here we go round the Mulberry Bush.
What big eyes you have Grand mama.
The Lion, the Witch and the Wardrobe.
Little Bo Peep she lost her sheep.

121 A B E H I.

122 Snake, Ache, Bake, Rake, Wake, Forsake, Lake, Break, Stake, Fake.

123 The Hobbit –
J.R.R. Tolkien
James and the Giant Peach
– Roald Dahl,
The House at Pooh Corner
– A.A. Milne
Finn Family Moomintroll
– Tove Jannson
Tom Sawyer – Mark Twain
White Fang – Jack London.

124 1. Rain
2. Sun
3. Snow
4. Hail.

125 Pimento. This is also the name of a food.

126 The correct order is wolf, taxi, hair, ache.
Fire is the thing which is hot.

127 To swim like a fish
To fly like a bird
To rain cats and dogs
To run like the wind
To smell like a rose.

128 Primrose
Buttercup
Daisy
Bluebell
Heather.

129 Rotate
Succulent
Dishwasher
Hostile
Nocturnal
Frontier
Lacerate
Unfurl
Misjudge
Quarterly

130 Saxophone.

131 Modicum
Cadmium
Academic
Dummied
Acceded.

132 Bugs, (all curved letters – no straight lines).

133
1. Harvard
2. Bangkok
3. Buttercup
4. Marsupial
5. Roulette
6. Diamond
7. Deciduous
8. Scotland
9. Cannibal
10. Planet.

134 Farmer
Fields
Horses
Cereal
Fences.

135 Sea of Tranquility.

136 Oblique
Infinity
Arrogance
Convalesce
Millennium
Subliminal
Humanoid
Ingenuity
Rudimentary
Bouquet.

137 Bill and Ted's Excellent
Adventure.
Around the World in
Eighty Days.
The Purple Rose of Cairo.
My Stepmother is an Alien.
The Importance of Being
Earnest.

138 See next page.

139 Loyal,
Spoil
Royal
Toil
Gargoyle.

140 Fridge
Microwave
Kettle
Oven
Saucer.

141 Disaster.

142 Blackguard
Blueberry
Blueprint
Blackbeard
Greenhouse

143 Ate pill.

144 Green Brian
(Big Ben, Old Glory,
Union Jack, Blue Beard
Stormin' Norman).

145 See over. Theme is the
word that appears twice.

146 First
Fist
Sift
Lift
Flit
Fit
Fig.

147 Tom Cruise.

148 Cat, Ant, Rat, Bat, Dog.

149 1. Just in time.
2. Cloud burst.
3. Isabel.
4. Shipwreck.
5. One thing after another.
6. Step by step.
7. Fiddler on the Roof.
8. The last resort.
9. Piggy in the middle.
10. Mixed nuts.
11. Young at Heart.
12. Jumble sale.
13. Rule the roost

150 E. (The second letter of
January, February,
March etc.)

151 The correct order is bird,
book, vase, chef.
The flower is rose.

152 Staple, Pastel, Palest,
Plates, Pleats, Petals.

153 Latin.

154 Bugle, Attack, Tank
Tactics, Lieutenant,
Enemy. The word is battle.

155 Mother Goose.

156 Elation, All, Slope, Pasta,
Red, Ordain, Barrier.
Breeds of Dog: Spaniel,
Poodle, Alsatian, Labrador,
Terrier.

157 1. Hockey.
2. Cycling.
3. Badminton.
4. Riding.
5. Karate.
6. Skating.

ANSWERS

158 Ski, Camp, Hail, Ocean, Olden, Lapel.
The answer is school.

159 1. Mansfield Park
– Jane Austen.
2. Hard Times
– Charles Dickens.
3. Romeo and Juliet
– William Shakespeare.
4. Tess of the d'Urbervilles
– Thomas Hardy.

160 Denmark, Iran, Canada, Germany, China.

161 Light
Spark
Shine
Gleam
Flame.

162 Igloo.

163 See over.
Janet Jackson is missing.

164 Electric, Longer, Ember, Cricket, Tablet, Rosemary, Oregano, Dawdle, Eternal.
The word is electrode.

165 A.

166 Teddy bear.

167 Cat, Dog, Fish, Hamster.

168 Laura, Freddy, Sally, Tony.

169 Too many chiefs and not enough Indians.
Many hands make light work.
An apple a day keeps the doctor away.

138

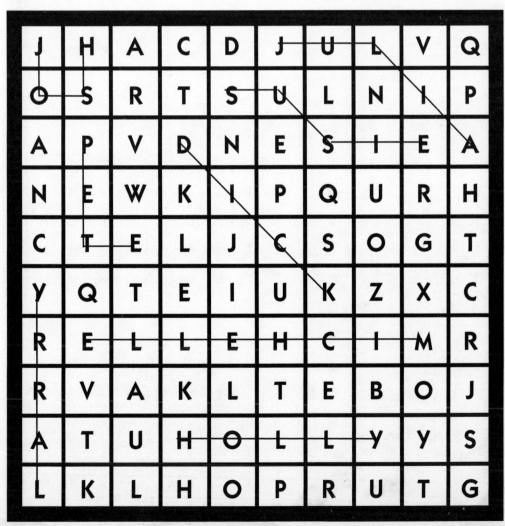

A new broom sweeps clean.
A stitch in time saves nine.
Cut your coat according to
your cloth.
When the cat's away the
mouse will play.
Can't see the wood for the
trees.
All's well that ends well.
It's an ill wind that blows.
nobody any good.

170 32.

171 Large elephants seldom
walk quickly.
Hamsters never take lunch
with crocodiles.
Even small giraffes sleep
standing.
Beautiful butterflies flitter
among flowers.
Giant pandas dwell among
bamboo groves.
All the words have their first
halves after their second.

145

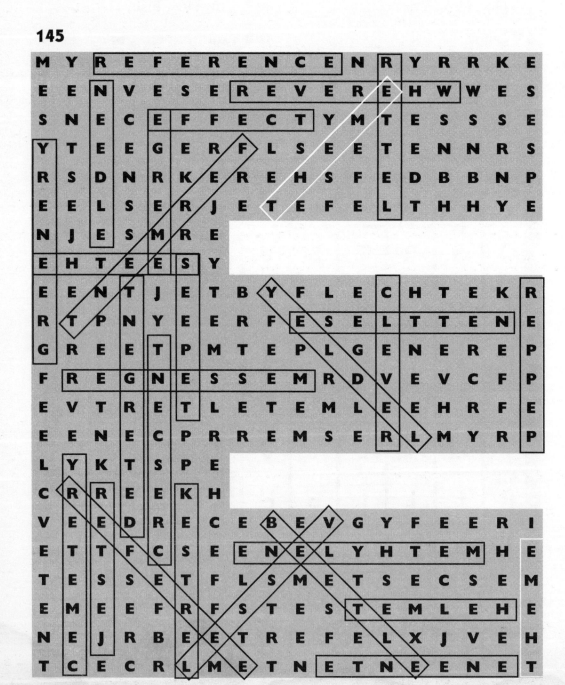

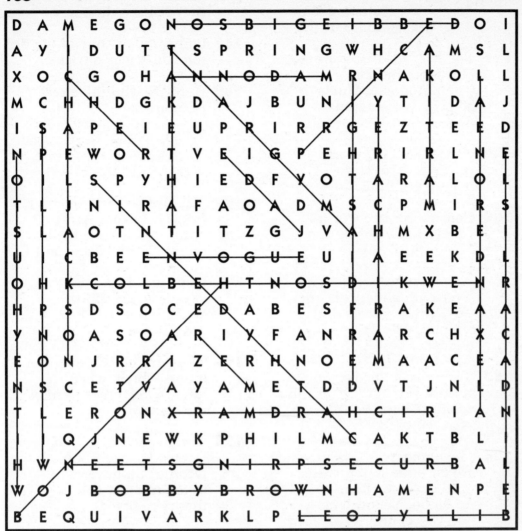

```
D A M E G O N O S B I G E I B B E D O I
A Y I D U T T S P R I N G W H C A M S L
X O C G O H A N N O D A M R N A K O L L
M C H H D G K D A J B U N Y T I D A J
I S A P E I E U P R I R R G E Z T E E D
N P E W O R T V E I G P E H R I R L N E
O I L S P Y H I E D F Y O T A R A L O L
T L J N I R A F A O A D M S C P M I R S
S L A O T N T I T Z G J V A H M X B E
U I C B E E N V O G U E U I A E E K D L
O H K C O L B E H T N O S D I K W E N R
H P S D S O C E D A B E S F R A K E A A
Y N O A S O A R I Y F A N R A R C H X C
E O N J R R I Z E R H N O E M A A C E A
N S C E T V A Y A M E T D D V T J N L D
T L E R O N X R A M D R A H C I R I A N
I I Q J N E W K P H I L M C A K T B L
H W N E E T S G N I R P S E C U R B A L
W O J B O B B Y B R O W N H A M E N P E
B E Q U I V A R K L P L E O J Y L L I B
```

172 1. It's an ill wind that blows nobody any good.
2. All work and no play makes Jack a dull boy.
3. Too many cooks spoil the broth.
4. You can't make a silk purse out of a sow's ear.
5. It never rains but it pours.

173 Bel (Bombay Duck, Catfish, Haddock, Piranha, Barracuda).

174 Vincent Van Gogh
Leonardo da Vinci
Pablo Picasso
John Constable
Marc Chagall.

175 Palace, Cottage, Bungalow, Castle, Monastery.

Cedar, Redwood, Hickory, Maple, Hornbeam.

176 The Wizard of Oz.
Close Encounters of the Third Kind.
Pollyanna.
Back to the Future.
National Velvet.
Batman Returns.
Beauty and the Beast.
Honey I Shrunk the Kids.
The Sound of Music.
Jurassic Park.

177 1. Twenty and Seven.
2. Million and One.
3. Three and Eight.
4. Two and Nine.
5. Four and Ten.

ANSWERS

178 Consonants are worth 3, vowels 12. Therefore Yale should be 30 miles away.

179 The five words (Average, Ear, Introduction, Onomatopoeia, Uncle) all begin with vowels. Ability fits.

180 Consonants are worth 7, vowels 8. Therefore Beijing is 53 miles away.

181 Consonants are worth 2, vowels 9. Therefore Essex is 24 miles away.

182 The letters are valued in reverse alphabetical order (A=26, B=25, etc) and multiplied by 10. Pancakes cost $14.60.

183 If you think this is going to be easy you had better think again. (All the vowels have been removed.)

184 The numbers above the line are all three-letter words.

185 All the words (Ready, Anything, Yellow, Analysis, Acolyte) contain Y. Heady fits.

186 When vertically reversed they remain the same.

187 Only one, of course. We did tell you it was a trick!

188 F, M, N. (Initial letters of months.

189 $7.80. A=1, B=2, C=3, etc. Then multiply the result by 10.

190 The five words (Anteater, Eagles, Ahead, Azalea, Nausea) all have EA in them. Confidence won't fit.

191 Consonants are worth 4, vowels 2, therefore Washington DC is 42 miles away.

192 They are all composed of letters which, when laterally reversed, remain the same.

193 The five words (Beach, Beans, Cease, Again, Drama) all have an A in the middle. Brass therefore fits.